Stage by Stage

A Life in Showbusiness

by Derek Grant

Published by MD Jones Books
mdjones303@outlook.com

Copyright © 2020 Derek Grant
All Rights Reserved

No part of this book may be reproduced, or stored in a retrieval system, or transmitted in any form or by any means, electronic, mechanical, photocopying, recording, or otherwise, without express written permission of the publisher.

Also by Derek Grant

Drama script

Charles Dickens' A Christmas Carol – One Man Show

Pantomime scripts
(with Michael Jones)

Goldilocks and the Three Bears

Treasure Island

The Ugly Duckling

Mother Goose

Humpty Dumpty and the Queen of Hearts

Aladdin and the Wonderful Lamp

Dick Whittington and his Cat

Little Red Riding Hood

The Owl and the Pussycat

Dedication

In loving memory of my parents Godfrey and Muriel,
and my brother Peter.

4

Stage by Stage
A Life in Showbusiness

Contents

Stage One: A Simple Childhood..11

Stage Two: Troubled Teens. 29

Stage Three: College, America, and on to Dorset................. 45

Stage Four: London University and Love. 93

Stage Five: Touring Puppeteer...123

Stage Six: Big Business in Showbusiness!..........................137

Stage Seven: Diversification and Change. 193

Stage Eight: Winding Down. 225

Stage Nine: Retirement?..249

APPENDIX 1: Sample children's/pantomime tour...........267

APPENDIX 2: Sample comedy/music tour.........................277

APPENDIX 3: Sample Reviews. 287

APPENDIX 4: International artistes seen on stage...........291

APPENDIX 5: UK artistes seen on stage..............................292

APPENDIX 6: Professional theatre booking terms..........293

Stage by Stage

"Life's a rum go, guv'nor, and that's the truth"

Dick Van Dyke as Bert the Chimney Sweep

"Life's a banquet, and most people are starving to death"

Patrick Dennis, from "Auntie Mame"

"Well God, here we are again"

Denis Janda, headmaster

"When you gonna wake up - and strengthen the things that remain?"

Bob Dylan

I was going to call this book "Three Score Years and Ten", because I was determined to finish it in time for my 70th birthday, and that is our allotted time on this earth.

However, my good friend Alun suggested a better title would be "A Disgrace to Anyone Living" in recognition of a remark he remembers made about me by my Great Aunt Mabel. You'll find out why she said this as you read on.

There have been those who've thought the way I've lived a lot of my life has been a disgrace, so that title would definitely be appropriate in their eyes!

However, I'm a positive sort of person, so I next thought I'd call it "Let Me Entertain You". That's a song from Gypsy by Stephen Sondheim, and it was also a hit for Robbie Williams. You see, whether it was putting on puppet shows as a small boy, producing big star-name theatre tours, or just holding a dinner party, I've always wanted to entertain. Standing in front of my classes of 11 year olds during my teaching days, or even just chatting at a bus stop, that's what I've tried to do.

But finally, I settled on Stage by Stage, because my life has had so many different stages. I had a simple, rather nervous childhood, followed by troubled teens, lacking in confidence. Then there was the college stage, and the stage when I was a teacher. The next stage was being a businessman, running a mail order business with my brother. Then there was the "coming out" stage which included meeting my true love, and that led on to the biggest stage in my life when I really was on stages all over the country!

Now as I write, I'm very much in the retirement stage, but involved in new interests which I'll tell you all about. As I'm fast approaching 70, I'm certainly well past middle age. Nevertheless, I certainly concur with Bob Monkhouse's remark. "Middle age is when you're offered two social engagements and you choose the one that'll get you home at 9 o'clock."

This is dedicated with thanks to <u>everyone</u> who has played a part in my life, so now, let me take you through my life – stage by stage.

10

Stage One: A Simple Childhood

In which I start school, we acquire a television set and a telephone, and I see my first pantomime.

1950

Harriet Harman, Joan Armatrading, Julie Walters, Princess Anne and Rowan Williams were born – and me!

Life started for me on the 12th of December (around 5.30 am I think) at Blighmont Nursing Home, Hill Lane, Southampton. My parents Muriel Sybil Webb (nee Bath) and Godfrey Edward Charles Webb took me home to live at 63 Prince of Wales Avenue in Regents Park, Southampton where we would reside until I was 14. My father was a Civil Servant – a draughtsman at the Ordnance Survey, and in those days that involved drawing the maps by hand. He would work with a magnifying glass, a brush or pen, and a bottle of Indian Ink meticulously writing place names in italics.

My mother was a housewife, having worked before their marriage as PA to Mr Haskins at Haskins Nursery in Ferndown. This was the business that became the modern-day Haskins Garden Centre, but when my mother worked there, Haskins occupied the site that is now a Sainsburys Supermarket.

I was baptised by Fr Stephenson at Holy Trinity Church, Millbrook as Christopher Charles Webb, Charles being one of my father's names as I've said, and also my grandfather's.

1951

The Festival of Britain was held on the South Bank near Waterloo Station, and Winston Churchill became Prime Minister again. I'm afraid I can't relate any memories of this year myself!

1952

Queen Elizabeth the Second came to the throne, disastrous floods engulphed Lynmouth in Devon, and the NME published the very first UK Singles Chart, which for the initial nine weeks was topped by Al Martino with "Here in my Heart", not that I was aware of it at the time.

1953

This was the year of the Coronation, and the year when Edward Hilary climbed Everest. My parents listened on the radio, as it would be several years before they were able to afford a television.

My own earliest memory, which I am told was of about 1953, is of going with my mother to a kind of depot where she was given powdered milk among other things, with rationing still being in place after the war. The door was at the top of a long flight of steps. That's all I can remember.

1954

Roger Bannister ran the four-minute mile, and I continued to live in Regents Park, Southampton. My mother was quite a mixture as a person, like we all are. One of the positive things about her was the education she gave me at home. She taught me basic maths and counting, and most of all, she taught me to read. This gave me a good grounding before I started school. We read Janet and John, and she bought me a subscription to the Enid Blyton Magazine, which came by post monthly. The newsagent delivered my weekly copies of Jack and Jill, and Playhour. Remember those?

<u>1955</u>

Birds Eye invented the frozen fish finger, and ITV was launched.

For me, this was the first really big change in my life. I started school at Regents Park Infants and my teacher was Mrs Horner. My main memory of her classroom was that the windows were so high that you couldn't look out of them, something deliberately done, no doubt, so that we wouldn't be distracted. I also remember the crates of little bottles of warm, gradually curdling milk which we were expected to drink each morning through paper straws (No plastic then!).

We had been on holiday in a caravan at White Sands Bay near Lands End in Cornwall. I think that was my very first holiday. This was also the first year I received pocket money. As I was 5 years old towards the end of 1955, my pocket money was 5d a week, 2p in today's money. This would go up to 6d on my 6th birthday, 7d on my 7th, etc. On my tenth birthday I received a bonus. Instead of 10d I had a shilling! (12 old pence, or five new.)

I can remember the first day at school, and being asked to draw a picture of "what I did in the holidays". I'm pretty sure Mrs Horner asked me something about it, and I said I had drawn the caravan I'd stayed in with mum, dad, and Peter my brother. Strange and sad to think I'm now the only one remaining of the four of us. Mrs Horner wrote a few words below the picture and I think we took our pictures home at the end of the day. Although I'd got underway quite well with reading, I don't think at that point I would have been capable of writing the caption, but that was the same for everyone in the class. There were almost forty of us four and five year olds for Mrs Horner to deal with!

Many years later, I myself, as a teacher, would start each term with getting my class to draw or write "what I did in the holidays".

1956

This was the year of the Suez Crisis and the beginning of Rock and Roll. Al Martino's "Here in my Heart" was long gone, and artistes like Elvis Presley were coming to prominence. I think it was around this time that we finally acquired a television. Up until then, we'd listened to the wireless, and I remember Children's Hour, Listen with Mother, Larry the Lamb – and then of course on the television, Sooty, who would play quite a large part in my life much later on.

When the television arrived, we turned it on at around 5.30 teatime, and Popeye was the first programme I ever watched.

<u>1957</u>

The famous Cavern Club opened in Liverpool and, keeping up with the latest trends as I always do, I acquired a hoola hoop. Not as easy as it might look! I think looking back, my distinct lack of ability when it came to swivelling my hips, was the first indication I was likely to be a thinker rather than a doer, and most definitely not much of a "mover"!

Whether that was a disappointment to my father he never said, although he himself was both a thinker and a doer. He could service car engines, make model steam locomotives that really worked, and write books that were acquired by international publishers.

My grandfather, Charles Webb, died at the age of 95. He had been a thoroughly good man, a carpenter, and a devoted husband to his wife Bess. They lived at 20 Wroxham Rd, Branksome, Poole.

Synchronicity is a theme of my life – and everyone's in fact. I've only recently learned to see this and once you do, you can see connections, insights you're being given, and lessons you're being taught.

Anyway, back to my grandparents' house at 20 Wroxham Rd. As I write now, over sixty years later, Michael and I have recently met and made friends with John and Judy Newbold, two of the main members of the William Temple Association in Bournemouth. They told me that their daughter had just been married and she and her young husband had bought a house in Branksome. It's number 20 Wroxham Rd!

<u>1958</u>

The first transatlantic passenger jetliner service began, and the European Common Market was formed. My mother's brother Eric and his family moved to Lytham St Annes near Blackpool. Uncle Eric, Auntie Marjorie and their daughters, my cousins Rosemary and Jennifer had been living in Salisbury. He was a branch manager for Eagle Star Insurance and had been promoted to the Blackpool branch. We had often visited them for Sunday afternoon tea at their home in Cambridge Rd, Salisbury.

Soon after their move, my father drove us all north to Lancashire to stay with them. Memories of trips away are becoming clearer now. I can remember being amused by the name "Ribble" on the buses around Preston, named after the river, and I was very taken with the funfair etc. on the seafront at Blackpool. Uncle Eric took me up the famous Tower, and bought me a comic to read. I got on well with my only uncle. He was full of life, interested in good music and the theatre. His favourite film was "High Society" with Bing Crosby, Frank Sinatra and Louis Armstrong and, as I have now discovered in another connection, this is one of my husband Michael's top favourite films as well.

<u>1959</u>

The M1 Motorway was opened, and postcodes were introduced.

I think it was around this time that we first had a telephone in the house. Until then, my mother would walk to the end of the road to a call box to phone the doctor or suchlike. Other memories of this time were waking up in my freezing cold bedroom with frost patterns on the <u>inside</u> of the windows, desperately trying to put off the moment when I'd have to step out of bed. With no carpet on the floor, only lino, your feet froze as they touched the shiny ice-cold surface with every step gingerly made towards the also-freezing bathroom.

I also recall waiting for the coalman to bring supplies. Big sacks of coal were stored in the coal shed near the back door, and all the soot that was created by our coal fires resulted in having to have the chimneys swept from time to time.

I have memories of sitting in a tin bath in front of one of those coal fires! The bath water was warm to begin with, but quickly cooled. Then there was the problem of stepping out again, shivering as you dried yourself. The heat from the fire was extremely localised, not extending very far into the room.

The sweep would come once a year, draping all the furniture with huge white cloths before he probed the extremities of the chimneys with his long brooms, bringing down big, black clouds of soot. I mentioned Dick Van Dyke at the very start of this book. Who can forget his Oscar-winning song and dance "Chim Chim Cheree" as cheerful chimney sweep Bert?

My grandmother on my mother's side, Granny Bath (Florrie) died. My mother Muriel went by train to Bournemouth when she received the news. She was so anxious to get there that she paid a supplement to travel on the Bournemouth Belle, which was the next train. Granny Bath was a very troubled soul. A constant hypochondriac, she spent much of her time in bed.

Grandad Bath (E Percy Bath) was a builder, running his own company. He built several of the big hotels at Westbourne in Bournemouth.

I guess I learned business skills from Grandad Bath. I also learned how not to treat your spouse! He would openly mock and disparage her, calling her "woman" when addressing her in front of other people. Mind you, she wasn't without faults herself, with her constant complaining.

Their house, on the main Ashley Rd through Upper Parkstone, was dark and foreboding. One room in particular was even more so.

My grandfather's office, if it is reasonable to call it that, was always dark. He kept the thick curtains drawn all the time, so you had to turn the light on to go in. It wasn't particularly disorderly, but certainly quite cluttered. The most striking feature was an enormous cobweb, made of thick string, which he'd strung across the whole ceiling, with a huge black woollen spider hanging in the middle. Nothing was ever explained, not his lack of taste in office furnishings, or the menu they served for us to eat _every_ time we visited.

Without fail, Grandad always served boiled ham with boiled potatoes and pickle, followed by tinned peaches and tinned cream. It was he who served the food, his wife being too unwell, depressed, disinterested or plain lazy to do any of it.

We are all the product of our upbringing, the experiences that life throws at us and, I guess, our genes. Grandad Bath would have been acutely aware of the terrible burdens men had to bear in those days. He'd served in the army in the first world war. He'd had to find a way to earn a living, and support his wife and children. He would have not found it easy or even possible to relate to me whom he wouldn't have seen as sufficiently masculine, with my puppet shows and love of Disney films and musicals. My grandfather used to call me "sissy" to my face. I knew it was an insult. I didn't really understand what it implied, but I knew it was a bad thing to be and it referred to me.

Grandad Bath had a brother, Uncle Arthur. He was a bachelor and rarely seen at family gatherings. Looking back, he was undoubtedly gay, but in those days that had to be carefully hidden. Hence his absence from family events.

We each have our own personal version of the general human pain and suffering. It's just our particular example of what everyone goes through. If we can't transmute our pain, we will surely transmit it.

Let me repeat that. If we can't transmute our pain, we will surely transmit it. In other words, we need to become aware of our own personal "baggage" and then come to terms with it. If we can find a way to transform it, we will be more able to find peace within ourselves and our dealings with others. When we fly off the handle with someone, or whatever, we're just passing on our pain - pain we haven't been able to deal with.

Certainly, a lot of what we suffer is passed on to us by our parents, unknowingly in the main. However, there's got to be a time when you realise what you do or say is your own affair. Seeing yourself, or your group as is so common nowadays, as a victim is a very unhealthy way to live.

I guess my brother Peter went to granny Bath's funeral with my parents, and I being too young was looked after by local friends of mum and dad.

1960 .

Sliced bread was widely introduced, and a sliced loaf cost about 10d (or 4p in today's money). The first edition of Coronation St was aired, which we watched with great interest. The idea of a "soap opera" was new. We'd seen weekly tv situation comedies like "I Love Lucy" and "Hancock's Half Hour" but this supposedly realistic ongoing drama was fascinating. It soon caught the nation's imagination and William Roach and his colleagues became stars.

My brother Peter went away to college at Cheltenham. St Paul's College was later to be a big influence on my own life but for now, I went with my parents in the car on several visits to see him there. It was at college that Peter was to meet Barbara, whom he would later marry.

Barbara would be his wife for 56 years until his tragic death in 2019. We read "for better or for worse" in the marriage service, and Barbara certainly lived up to that ideal, remaining faithful and loving to the very end, visiting him every single day during his final long decline. They never moved, living in the same house in Athelstan Road in Southampton throughout their long marriage.

I love to travel, mainly within the British Isles. My brother loved to stay put. I love the arts. My brother liked science and maths. I am garrulous. My brother was a man of fewer words.

It was in 1960 that we first acquired a reel to reel tape recorder. My father took advantage of a discount for civil servants, and we drove to Newbury to pick it up. I can remember my parents recording the soundtrack of various television shows by placing a microphone near the tv's loudspeaker. Dad recorded a performance by George Formby (I think his last) and mum recorded a programme featuring the Beverley Sisters. Many years later, The Bevs would work for Michael and me in our Summer Season at the West Cliff Theatre, Clacton, a season in which we also incidentally included a George Formby tribute artiste, Andy Eastwood! There are always so many connections in each of our lives. Those were some of the first connections for me.

I was given my own reel of tape, to record what I wanted. I enjoyed the Sunday lunchtime shows on the Light Programme and, whereas most people seemed to be keen on Hancock's Half Hour or The Navy Lark, my favourite was Life with the Lyons. Looking back, I can now see I preferred the American style of wisecrack humour, rather than the British "everyman" underdog, epitomised by Tony Hancock and the like.

My father had two main interests – railways and gypsies. This was the year that both significantly moved forward.

Firstly, the Bluebell line, as it was called, from East Grinstead to Lewes in West Sussex was closed to passengers and about to be lifted. This was before the famous Beeching Report three years later. Enthusiasts, spurred on by the success of efforts to save the Talyllyn narrow gauge line in Wales, decided to try to save a standard gauge branch line. We went over there several times to Sheffield Park and, as a little boy of 9, I helped to paint one of the carriages.

Gypsies were the subject of my father's first book, published by Herbert Jenkins, "Gypsies the Secret People". It was quite something to have my father on tv and radio being interviewed about this and, for many years after, whenever the BBC had a feature about gypsies, they would telephone him for a comment.

In 1960, I was taken to my first pantomime, Mother Goose, at the Grand Theatre, Southampton. Long gone, the site of the old theatre is now a shopping centre. Now even that is struggling to survive.

Mother Goose starred Joan Regan and Richard Hearne as Mr Pastry. Amazingly, Joan would go on to work for Michael and me in one of our seaside Summer Seasons in 2003. Making his professional debut as the young comic Silly Billy was Terry Scott. We were sitting near the front, and towards the end, for what they call the "song sheet", the Dame asked children to come up on the stage and help. I didn't give it a second thought! I ran up the steps, and was soon taking part in "Old MacDonald Had a Farm". My abiding memory is looking at the audience there in the darkness, and the amazing contrast between us performers in the bright lights on the stage in front of all the colourful scenery, and looking out into the wings into another world of apparent busyness in the shadows. I wanted to explore that world – both worlds, the one on the stage and the one in the wings.

Strangely, Mother Goose was to be my first pantomime and, in a way, my last, because it was the title of the last professional pantomime Michael and I produced at Christmas 2009. But I'm getting ahead of myself. More about that later!

1960 was the year that I won the cake competition at our local church. My mother taught me how to make a madeira cake, but the cake I entered was definitely "all my own work" as they say. Each cake was cut, and mine was pronounced as having the most moist and consistent texture. There was much discussion around the fact that I was a boy, and only girls were supposed to be good at cakes!

<u>1961</u>

Yuri Gagarin was the first man in space, and self-service supermarkets opened. We went to Tesco and found you could walk round the store just taking things from the shelves yourself, rather than having to ask for them from an assistant behind the counter. This meant that you ended up buying much more than you would have done, which of course was the whole idea!

Up until then, my mother had bought all our groceries at Bax's Grocers at the top of our road, Prince of Wales Avenue. You asked Mr Bax for what you wanted and he got it off the shelves and wrapped it for you, maybe weighing it first, or in the case of bacon or ham, slicing it.

Did I just say slicing? I should point out that Mr Bax had the top of one of his fingers missing. True!

There were no safety features on bacon slicers in those days. You were expected to be careful, which I'm sure he generally was. However, just one slight slip ...

I'm sure you remember that Russ Conway played piano so well with just nine fingers, the same fate having befallen him during his time in the navy as ship's cook.

I had become very interested in theatre and performance, and especially puppets. There was Sooty, as I said, but I'd been to see various puppet shows with marionettes that were performed in the school holidays, and on the tv we had Pinky and Perky, two cute little marionette pigs. I made a couple of puppets myself – a glove puppet mouse, and a string puppet Gepetto. My parents could see that this was a great interest of mine and my father made me a puppet theatre, while my mother sewed costumes, curtains etc.

My mother gave piano lessons privately at home in our front room, to provide a bit of extra income. My father's wages were low at the Ordnance Survey, and a little extra would help. She attempted (and failed) to teach me to read music. I'm ashamed to say I just didn't try. I suppose you don't have respect for your teacher when she's your own mother, and to this day I still can't play from printed music. I can busk a few tunes, as could my father, but that's about it.

"A prophet is not without honour, save in his own country", or in my mother's case "hers".

This was certainly a time when my father was busy and creative. He founded the Hampshire Narrow Gauge Railway Society, which had the aim of restoring part of the Bishops Waltham branch, near Botley. The initial idea had been to revive part of the Alton to Fareham line, starting from West

Meon station, but this proved impractical. We started to go frequently on Sunday afternoons to view the trackbed, etc. and on Wednesday evenings to the Railway Institute, Eastleigh for society meetings. Two narrow gauge engines, Wendy and Cloister, were brought from the redundant slate quarries in North Wales to Fair Oak near Southampton for restoration. The society continued for several years, but never developed beyond the small industrial site at Fair Oak. Disagreements and clashing personalities and generations caused my father to resign as Chairman. Over the years and subsequent decades, we read about the further exploits of the organisation which remained very modest. It became a Trust which was only disbanded in 2020, the few assets, amazingly including those first two engines we'd brought from North Wales, being dispersed at that point.

This was the year when I stayed for the first time at a hotel. We went to Sandown on the Isle of Wight, and stayed at a small private guest house on the front. Until then, we'd only been able to afford to stay in a caravan once a year. I took part in a talent competition, went through several heats and the semi-final during the week, and then finally won! I was presented with a set of wooden skittles which I still have. What did I do for my act? I performed The Lion and Albert by Marriot Edgar, made famous by Stanley Holloway.

One morning we woke up in our seafront room, pulled back the curtains and saw the famous vintage car Genevieve on the promenade opposite. It was the actual one from the film and was there for a promotion of some kind.

We went on the British Rail train to Ventnor and back, a line which was to be partially closed soon after, cut back to Shanklin where it still terminates today. You got out at the end of the line at Ventnor and found yourself about a thousand feet above sea level, at the very back of the town. It was all right walking down to the front, zigzagging through various roads, walkways and steps, but it was walking back UP to the train after your day on the beach that was the problem! Could that be part of the reason for closing that bit of the line?

Stage Two: Troubled Teens.

In which I begin to feel "different", start my night terrors, and earn my first ten shillings in showbusiness!

1962

Marilyn Monroe died, and the Beatles released their first single "Love Me Do".

I took the 11 Plus and gained a place at King Edward VI School, Southampton. This was a boys only, direct grant grammar school. I'm not sure what the direct grant bit actually meant, but the overriding memory is of a period of great fear. We certainly had a wonderful education, but it was delivered in an atmosphere of terror! Seven years of great anxiety, during which I came to realise (a) I was different from the rest of the boys, and (b) this was something that I must do my utmost to hide at all times.

My mother would often take me to coffee at Mayes Department Store in Southampton, and I was very taken with the pianist who would play there every morning. Just about my favourite performing artiste at that time was Russ Conway, who had numerous hit records and was frequently on tv in his own series, and on the Billy Cotton Band Show. This handsome man had something about him, as far as I was concerned, and I felt just the same way about the good looking young pianist at Mayes store. I was terribly upset to read in the local paper that he had been sacked from his job at the coffee lounge due, it said, to an encounter with another young man. I couldn't understand what the paper meant (I think you can probably guess), and I asked my mother why we wouldn't see him any more. She just said "he turned out to be a nasty man". I couldn't enquire any further but deep inside I felt something of an affinity with the talented pianist, but I didn't know what it was. What I DID wonder was whether I was going to grow up to be a nasty man as well.

I soon made friends at school with Stephen Lee, who would become a lifelong friend, and who would also go on to work extremely successfully in professional showbusiness. My other friend was Brian Hinton, who would become an art gallery curator on the Isle of Wight, and an authority on Bob Dylan!

1963

The notorious Beeching Report was published, resulting in the closure of around a third of our railways and over two thousand stations. Locally we lost services from Southampton to Ringwood, West Moors and Wimborne, Southampton to Andover via Stockbridge, and Southampton to Marchwood, Hythe and Fawley. Not far away, most of the West Country branch lines were closed such as those to Lyme Regis, Seaton, Sidmouth, Padstow, etc.

Unknown to me, this was the year that Michael, my husband to be, was born in Corby, Northants.

It was also the year that my brother Peter married his fiancé Barbara Smith. She was from Kenilworth, Warwickshire. We all travelled up there for the wedding and I sat next to my grandmother Bess for the lunch. She and I both said what nice chicken soup it was. When they told us it had been mushroom, we were both amazed as neither of us liked mushrooms!

I think my brother's was the first of many weddings I would attend over the years, never for one minute imagining I would eventually attend my own.

Do you remember the fictional young bride-to-be discussing her forthcoming wedding with her mother?

"Mummy, I DO want everything to be perfect. I'm determined not to overlook even the most insignificant little detail."

"Don't worry dear. I'll make sure your father is there."

And thinking of fathers reminds me that my father's second book was published that year, a novel about gypsy life called "Tom Hathaway".

<u>1964</u>

Harold Wilson became Prime Minister. His party had promised to reverse many of the Beeching cuts but in the event, once elected, they went on to close even more of our railways, not just branch lines this time, but hundred-mile-long main lines which would be much needed today.

My grandmother Bess (Grandma Webb) married again. She had been on her own at Wroxham Rd since the death of my grandfather seven years earlier, and during this time she had been renting out a second property they owned in Alby Rd nearby. Her tenant was John Stimson, a widower. They became friendly and decided to marry for companionship. My grandmother moved in with him at Alby Rd, and sold the Wroxham Rd house.

This was quite a year, entertainment-wise. The BBC began broadcasting Top of the Pops, and two or three months into the run, I started to watch regularly. One particular programme ended with "I Believe" by The Bachelors. Several other groups had sung, but that was all they did. They just stood and sang their song.

The Bachelors were different. They had real "presence" and charisma. Their performance was properly staged, powerful and theatrical, and I became a fan. I started to listen on Sunday afternoons to Pick of the Pops, and got to like Alan Freeman, and of course The Bachelors were there every week as well, with their songs often going higher in the charts than records by groups like The Searchers, The Rolling Stones and even The Beatles.

I had a transistor radio of my own by then, and on one memorable Sunday afternoon, we went to Badbury Rings near Wimborne for a picnic, mum, dad, Peter, Barbara, and me. "Ramona" had just entered the top ten, and that was the first time I heard it, out in the open Dorset air at Badbury Rings.

Remember Charmaine, Marie, Marta, and of course the number one hit Diane? "Smile for me ...!"

How could I ever have imagined back then that fifty or more years later I would still often be walking round Badbury Rings with my husband Michael. It's just about our favourite local walk here in Dorset and we have many.

By the way, please indulge my references to The Bachelors who will be very significant in my story later on.

This was the year that Mary Poppins premiered at the cinemas. Undoubtedly Walt Disney's greatest achievement, it was conceived as an original Broadway musical on film. Winner of several Oscars, it introduced me to Julie Andrews who rightly won Best Actress, and the music of The Sherman Brothers, who won two Oscars - Best Original Musical Score and Best Original Song (Chim Chim Cheree). It's a piece of theatre, with stunning choreography, great characterisations from world class actors, and intelligent, thoughtful and witty dialogue.

Also in 1964, we went away to stay at Llandudno in North Wales. We discovered my television favourite Russ Conway was appearing at the Pier Pavilion, and went to see him. This was my first time at a Summer Show and I was smitten by the whole production with the dancing girls, the orchestra, the support acts, and the top-of-the-bill.

This was the year that saw the launch of Crossroads. It was conceived as a vehicle for Noele Gordon. She had hosted ATV's daily variety show Lunch Box for a decade or more, but variety was on the way out, and Coronation Street was leading the way into the nation's love of "Soaps". Set in a fictional midlands motel with Noele as proprietor Meg Richardson, the very first line of the very first Crossroads episode was uttered by Jane Rossington who played Jill, Meg's daughter. She picked up the phone in the motel's reception and said "Crossroads Motel, may I help you?" and television history was made!

45 years later, Michael and I cast Jane Rossington in the title role of our drama production of The Snow Queen. What a lovely lady, and what a talented actress, much loved by audiences everywhere we went.

With the problems I've described at the Hampshire Narrow Gauge Railway, my father wanted to find a way to express his love of steam railways. He had made friends with a man called Bert Merritt who had a miniature 10" gauge locomotive. This could pull short trains carrying about twelve people at a time who sat astride the track which was on short stilts. The whole thing was portable, and Bert would get bookings to run his trains at fetes, etc. In summer '64, I went regularly with my father to help with some of these events and was sometimes even allowed to drive the engine. We ran it in the park at Eastleigh, a railway town in those days, as part of a fun fair there.

<u>1965</u>

The miniskirt was invented, the national speed limit of 70 mph was introduced, and Winston Churchill died.

For us, this was quite a year. My grandfather on my mother's side, E Percy Bath also passed away aged 78. This brought about quite a change as my mother received an inheritance. Grandad's estate was divided equally between my mother and her brother, my Uncle Eric. With this money, we were able to afford to move to a bigger and better house, and this was how we came to live in Shirley Avenue.

Fr Stephenson, at Holy Trinity Church, retired and was replaced by Fr Moon, who was more "high church" than his predecessor. Although we had moved further away, it was only about three miles to Millbrook and, as we were all very taken with Fr Moon and his ministry, we continued to worship at Holy Trinity. I started confirmation classes with Fr Moon. I think there were twelve or thirteen sessions, held weekly. Then on Nov 7th I was confirmed by the Bishop of Winchester, at Winchester Cathedral. I still have the World Atlas that my grandmother Bess (Grandma Webb) gave me to commemorate the date. She had been my Godparent.

I took my first Holy Communion, which meant a tremendous amount to me. I have a vivid recollection of kneeling by the altar rail and looking up at the stained glass window in front of me with the light streaming down. I loved the majesty of the organ music, the singing of the traditional hymns, and the poetry of the words.

I think it was around this time that I started my night terrors. I would regularly wake around 3.00 am in the midst of terrible screaming, usually dreaming of being attacked, often by one or more black dogs leaping up at me. This would leave me shaken and quaking with fear, too afraid to go back to sleep. These dreams would go on for the next fifty years or more, certainly decreasing in frequency, but it would often take just the slightest thing to trigger another attack. I don't recall them happening while I was away at college at Cheltenham, and I don't recall them during my year living in London in my 30s, but they returned once I was on home territory again at Southampton or where I was teaching in Bournemouth.

Looking back, I can see what the problem was, and I expect you can as well.

The great fear of attack was based on my fully understandable fear of being discovered as "queer", and the consequences that could result from that. Lord Montagu and many others had been publicly shamed, humiliated, and actually imprisoned for completely consensual behaviour between adults. I was pretty near being discovered myself, with my own grandfather, Grandad Bath, calling me a sissy to my face.

This was also the year of The Sound of Music. It ran at cinemas for months on end, preventing the showing of other new pictures. My great aunt Mabel went to see it 26 times (along with many others all over the country) and I went twice myself. Everyone was smitten.

In my introduction, I mentioned her remark "a disgrace to anyone living". She wasn't referring to me as a whole, but merely my shoes. In a sad attempt to keep up with fashion (something I've not tried since), I was wearing platform shoes and she clearly didn't approve.

She was happy in general with what I was wearing, she said, but "the shoes are a disgrace to anyone living", the implication being that people who had died wouldn't be shocked by the sight of them – a notion it would be hard to disagree with.

Peggy Lee has always been one of my favourite singers. I wouldn't have said she looked in any way untoward, but Great Aunt Mabel, when visiting one time and being confronted with Peggy on the Andy Williams Show, exclaimed "Just LOOK at her!" Certainly, our Peg was giving us one of her sultry looks, trying her best to look sufficiently seductive while singing Fever, but it really was quite slight when compared to what we see on television today.

Still in entertainment, but on a much smaller scale, my own puppet theatre was "opened" by my sister-in-law Barbara on 1 February. My first production was Pinocchio which I performed with marionettes. Some were the famous Pelham Puppets which my parents had given me and some were my own creation. 40 years later, Michael and I would tour two different productions of Pinocchio to UK theatres, our final tour starring tv's Crackerjack comedian Don Maclean as Gepetto.

We went on holiday to a small guest house at Fairbourne on the Cambrian Coast. I think a major attraction for my father was that it had its own miniature railway which ran out to Penrhyn Point from where you could catch the ferry across to Barmouth. You could also get the "big" British Rail train to Barmouth across the famous bridge. Almost a mile long, it has 115 wooden supports, and there is a walkway alongside the railway line from where you can see some of the most spectacular views in Wales, looking up the Mawddach Estuary towards Dolgellau. We took the train one day, and found a queue at the ticket office at Fairbourne Station. The clerk was complaining to everyone that British Rail had not sent him any stocks of cardboard tickets and he had completely run out. This meant that he had to write each ticket out by hand on a paper voucher, keeping a carbon copy for a record!

Needless to remark, there is no ticket office at Fairbourne Station today. Under the general "improvements" to our railways, the only remaining facility is a bus-shelter type construction on the single platform. You have to buy your ticket on the train, that's if anyone comes along to sell you one!

The train to Barmouth stopped at Morfa Mawddach. This had recently been renamed. It had been Barmouth Junction until the sad closure of the line from there across to Bala, Corwen, Llangollen and Ruabon. Now it was no longer a junction, hence the renaming. The refreshment room was still open however, on the platform between the lines, and we had morning coffee there a few times.

In years to come, Morfa Mawddach would have great significance in my life. I would take several parties of children there during residential visits, I named my house at Corfe Mullen "Morfa Mawddach", and Michael and I would visit many times to take the spectacular walk across the bridge. The station is still open, as a request stop halt. Such is progress!

When December came around, Barbara, who was teaching at Hedge End Infants School near Southampton, telephoned to say that the conjuror they were to have for the end-of-term entertainment was unable to come. She thought my puppet show was absolutely of a standard to be performed to a wider audience than the few uncles, aunts and friends who'd seen it in our front room, and wondered if I'd like to go and perform it for her school. My father asked my headmaster Dr Stroud for permission for me to go, Peter agreed to drive me there, and the deal was done.

On the day, it all went very well and the headmistress was very pleased. What I had never considered was that the conjuror would have been paid. She gave me the ten shillings that she would have given to him, and I thereby earned my first fee in professional showbusiness!

<u>1966</u>

The first credit card was introduced by Barclays Bank and called Barclaycard. The Severn Bridge was opened, and also in Wales the Aberfan disaster claimed the lives of many.

John Lennon declared that the Beatles were now bigger than Jesus.

My father started building his own 10" gauge steam locomotives. The beauty of model making is that you can do it all yourself in entirely your own way. This he found most satisfying.

Walt Disney died, just after completing what was to be his last film, "The Happiest Millionaire", a lavish, Oscar-winning musical based on the Broadway play of the same name.

Again, on a much smaller scale, my own puppet shows continued to expand. Along with my friend Stephen Lee, we produced a puppet pantomime of Cinderella which Father Moon invited us to perform in the Church Hall. We then took this to other churches and charities, with my uncomplaining father providing the transport, and even enlarging the theatre itself so that it needed a trailer to carry it. The collaboration with Stephen didn't last, with him leaving school and going away to work at Staines, and me carrying on at King Edward VI into the sixth form. I had gained eight O Levels, failing a ninth – History.

I produced another puppet panto on my own, Aladdin, but this was a pale imitation of Cinderella without Stephen's input, and I quickly moved to a more "cabaret" style of solo presentation.

My Uncle Eric and Aunt Marjorie moved back from Lancashire to live much nearer to us at Barnham near

Chichester. Now we could regularly visit them again. They had a lovely home - "Cherry Tree Cottage".

We went on holiday once more to the small guest house at Fairbourne, visiting the Talyllyn and Ffestiniog railways and even journeying by car right up to Rhos on Sea, near Colwyn Bay on the north coast, where there was Britain's only purpose-built, permanent puppet theatre. Eric Bramall performed a marionette cabaret every afternoon, including his own creation "Le Ballet Mouchoir". Visiting this show certainly spurred me on to greater things with my own puppets, and it was wonderful of my parents to give me so much encouragement.

1967

The Sexual Offences Act partially decriminalised consensual homosexual behaviour between adults, and Jeremy Thorpe became leader of the Liberal Party.

The Abortion Act was passed.

Barclays, again the trendsetter, introduced the ATM – a "cash point" machine, soon to be known as the "hole in the wall". As the ubiquitous Pirate Radio stations were sunk, the BBC Radio's Light Programme and Home Service came to an end, to be replaced by Radios One, Two, Three and Four.

Not keen on Radio One, I soon became a daily listener of Radio Two with the morning Pete Murray's Open House and the lunchtime Jimmy Young Show. I enjoyed the programmes of David Jacobs, Sam Costa, Desmond

Carrington, and of course Saturday Club with Brian Matthew. A different world to look back on now.

Sandie Shaw won the Eurovision Song Contest for Great Britain with "Puppet on a String".

Thinking of puppets on strings, that reminds me to relate the progress, or otherwise, I was making with my own puppet cabaret.

Mostly, I appeared at clubs, hotels, etc., numerous church halls, and the department stores I've already mentioned, with my parents providing the transport. I wrote my own advertising leaflets and found names and addresses in the Yellow Pages to mail these out to, resulting in lots and lots of bookings.

This was a real learning curve. Whereas initially, the puppets performed and Stephen and I were hidden behind the scenes, now I was on stage with them. I had to "engage" with the audience of children and adults. Embarrassment is hardly the word when you have to soldier on to the end of your well-rehearsed hour, sensing disinterest at best, or occasionally real opposition!

I kept going, never wanting to give up, only to try to improve. It's a good job that I wasn't familiar back then with Quentin Crisp's famous line, "If at first you don't succeed, failure may be your style".

I worked at my act, honing and tuning it in light of the feedback I was getting, and in the long run this stood me in good stead, as the comment Michael and I got more than any other when we were producing all kinds of professional theatre shows several decades later was that we'd "held" the audience captivated throughout the presentation.

I entered the sixth form to study three A Levels – English Literature, Art and Divinity (what would now be called Theology). There were only the two of us on the Divinity course, my friend Brian Hinton and myself. Our tutor was George Rust, an eccentric bachelor with an absolutely encyclopaedic knowledge of the Bible. I just about coped with the Art course and scraped through the Art A Level with a pass. I did better with Theology and English, gaining three A Levels altogether.

This was a joyful time for Peter and Barbara as their first daughter, my niece Rachel was born on 22 August. My father made a humorous film "New Arrival" mixing animation with live action scenes of the new baby.

Once I had turned 17 in the December, I was able to begin driving lessons. My parents had generously given me a course of 20 lessons as my 17th birthday present.

<u>1968</u>

Demonstrations were held in London regarding American involvement in the Vietnam War, and Enoch Powell made his controversial "rivers of blood" speech.

The Race Relations Act and the Trades Descriptions Acts were passed, and the Theatres Act ended much of the censorship of stage plays, quickly followed by the opening of the musical "Hair".

5p and 10p coins were introduced, replacing the shilling and florin, as a step towards decimalisation.

I passed my driving test in the Spring, but it would be many years until I would be able to afford a car. My father generously let me drive myself to my puppet show bookings in his car. Everything for my cabaret-style show now fitted into the boot and the back seat area of his Ford Cortina. (Remember those?)

Which leads me to the hoax booking.

As well as sending out leaflets to clubs and hotels, I'd started paying for adverts in the local Echo, and as a result was booked for a birthday party at a private house, the kind of thing that would most likely be quite a steep learning curve! Anyway, I didn't get the chance to learn how to handle a difficult audience on their own home ground as I arrived to find the address didn't exist, and I'd been tricked.

I never knew who'd carried out the hoax, or why, but that was one Saturday afternoon of my teenage years well and truly wasted!

We went on holiday to Peel on the Isle of Man, travelling on the ferry from Liverpool. I saw the famous Liver Building as we waited at the dock, and on the island, I saw the Laxey Wheel.

Stage Three:
College, America, and on to Dorset.

In which I leave home to study theology at Cheltenham, teach in America, and move to Bournemouth.

<u>1969</u>

On July 20th, Neil Armstrong became the first man on the moon. Grandma Webb said it couldn't have happened and it was all set up in the tv studio.

The death penalty was abolished, and the Beatles announced their split. The 50p coin was introduced replacing the ten shilling note, and Prince Charles was invested as Prince of Wales at Caernarfon Castle.

Stephen and I (separately) joined the World Record Club. You had to be 18, which we now were. You could buy lp records by post, with the first three at giveaway prices. The arrangement was that you would then agree to buy at least five more each year at full price. My first selections included "Russ Conway at the Cinema", lush orchestral arrangements from Tony Osborne and his Orchestra with Russ at the piano, and "Tommy Steele – So This is Broadway".

I still have my "Russ Conway at the Cinema", now digitally remastered on cd, and play it often as one of my all-time favourites. I remember one of Stephen's first choices was Harry Secombe in "Pickwick". Tommy Steele has just now, as I write in 2020, been made Sir Tommy!

As I've, hopefully, matured, so have my tastes. Nowadays I really appreciate today's great world-class artistes like the incredible young pianist Lang Lang, and outstanding violinist Nicola Benedetti. From the past, I love the piano music of Oscar Peterson, and one of my favourite albums now is "Charlie Parker with Strings". However, for happy nostalgia and security, I still turn to Russ Conway, and what's wrong with that?

Although I credit Grandad Bath and his like as being part of the problem that caused my night terrors, I must acknowledge what I clearly inherited from him – his entrepreneurship. I had no confidence or interest whatsoever around the idea of finding a girlfriend, but I was able at the age of 18 to take myself off to Edwin Jones Department Store to do a deal with the manager to put on my cabaret style puppet shows for a fortnight during the school holidays. This proved a great success and was followed by similar seasons I negotiated at Debenhams at Salisbury. I was soon asked to provide my puppet cabaret at "Breakfast with Santa" at Christmastime as well.

My mother was tremendously supportive of my shows in her own way, making costumes for the puppets, and sewing curtains for the stage. She always said how astounding it was one day when she came to see one of my shows at Debenhams. Her voice was on the taped soundtrack, playing one of the puppet characters. I repeated the show nine times each day at 45 minute intervals. When she'd seen a performance in the theatre they'd made for me on the top floor, she went back down to the street to catch the bus home. While waiting at the bus stop, she could pick up her own voice coming down from the open window way up above!

Amazing now in 2020 that Debenhams Department Store in Southampton is no more. I walked past the other day. The huge building is closed, with a few forlorn notices remaining, offering 2 for the price of 1 items, and toasted sandwiches in the forever abandoned coffee shop.

More connections ... "Open Window" was the title my mother gave to her correspondence magazine for women. It was a kind of round robin which she sent out each month to twelve members. Everyone added a new letter giving their personal news plus opinions on current affairs, and removed their previous one. You could add comments on other people's contributions and so it was a lively, thriving affair. She organised it beautifully, and it went out on the first of each month like clockwork. Have you ever heard of Facebook? In a way, my mother's scheme was a bit of a forerunner of today's social media. Mind you, my mother didn't "monetise" her members by selling every tiny detail about their lives and interests to anyone who would pay, and her magazine was updated every month, not every few seconds!

In the summer, we went on holiday to Fort William in the Scottish Highlands. This involved a long drive up the M6 Motorway, and an overnight stay at Carlisle. Being quite used to Wales, I was struck by the different style of towns in Scotland. We travelled on the steam train to Mallaig, and went "over the sea to Skye".

This was the year of a great change as I went away to college at Cheltenham.

Just before my father drove me there in September, my parents took me to see The Bachelors at Bournemouth Winter Gardens. In those days the summer shows were performed to two houses each night. We went to first house at 6.10 and there was a "house full" of around 1000 people. When we came out there were another thousand people queuing outside three or four deep all down the road, waiting to go in to second house!

It was a real treat, and so kind of my parents, as The Bachelors were my firm favourites by then and I had never seen them on stage before. There was a twelve piece orchestra with them and it was a wonderful show, with several guest artistes including ventriloquist Ray Alan and Lord Charles.

The Winter Gardens is now no more, having been demolished to make way for yet another car park. It had a particularly wide stage, ideal for the Bournemouth Symphony Orchestra, and excellent acoustics. Bulldozed. Razed to the ground.

My college, St Paul's was a Church of England College and I studied Divinity (Theology), Art, and Primary Education. This was the same college that Peter had attended ten years earlier to study science and maths.

I quickly made friends with what became our "group" – Bob England (who was a Methodist), Roger Wheelhouse (Baptist), Roger Welshman (C of E), Alun Williams (Plymouth Brethren), and Bill Ives (C of E). I had to share a room in Hall and my room-mate was John Kidney, from Northampton. He was another Anglican.

Although I was extremely nervous about leaving home, I soon became really well settled. I loved Cheltenham as a place, and the whole Cotswolds area. I came to like Gloucester, nine miles away, and frequently visited the Cathedral, also Tewkesbury with its famous Abbey. Our little group would often go out into the Cotswolds on Saturday afternoons to places like Stow on the Wold, Winchcombe, Broadway, etc.

Our group's very first evening out together was to the Playhouse Theatre for "An Evening with Anthony Hopkins". He spoke about his favourite classical music and played records. The stage was set with a coffee table and flowers, plus a soft, easy chair with wooden arms. This would be just the kind of thing Michael and I would present forty years later when we started doing our "Evenings With …" celebrity shows.

When Anthony arrived on stage he sat down on one of the wooden arms of the chair rather than in the seat itself. As he settled his buttocks precariously on the rather narrow arm, the first thing he said was "Disregarding the advantages of G-Plan ..." and then launched into his patter. I've always remembered this, as the very first line of any show is so very important. You set the tone for all that is going to follow, although some would say, to quote the song, "It's not how you start, it's how you finish!"

After only a fortnight at College, we were sent out on our first teaching practice. Bob England and I were at Painswick Primary School, both in the same class, with teacher Miss Page. This was the top class, 11 year olds, and one of the children was Laurie Lee's daughter. I greatly enjoyed the experience and we made friends with Miss Page, going back to visit on several occasions.

For my birthday in December, Stephen Lee took me to Jerry Herman's musical "Mame" at the Theatre Royal, Drury Lane, starring Ginger Rogers. It was a follow-up to his huge hit with "Hello Dolly!" a few years earlier. This was my first time at a West End show and I was "blown away" as they say nowadays! A particular memory I have of the show, which was a matinee, was that you could order afternoon tea to be brought to your seats in the interval. This cost half a crown (13p in today's money). We were near the front in the stalls and a woman pushed past us to get to her seat further down the row. As she went by, Stephen tapped her on the shoulder and said "Excuse me, this is my left foot. Would you like to stamp on that one as well?"

I also continued my own very small-scale performances with my puppet cabaret, playing at children's parties, Working Men's Clubs, British Legions, churches and charities. This produced a good income to support me through college, and my parents provided financial support as well (no grants).

<u>1970</u>

Peter and Barbara's second daughter was born - my niece Nina.

The New English Bible was published.

Life at college continued. I did a second teaching practice at Watermoor Primary School, Cirencester with Mr Braine's class of 11 year olds. Again, I enjoyed this very much and, like I had done at Painswick, I went back to visit Mr Braine and the children several times, even going with them on a day trip to London.

Only a short time after this, I received a letter in the post from Mr Braine's wife, telling me that he had been thrown from a horse and killed, and that she was now a widow.

The age of majority was reduced from 21 to 18. As many of my college friends had already passed 18, but had not yet reached 21, some of us decided to still go ahead with 21st birthday parties when the dates came round.

For this second year, we had to move out of Hall and find our own accommodation. Bob England and I rented a small cottage on the edge of Cheltenham. He had a car, being eight years older and a "mature" student, so he could drive us into town.

Lunch for us non-resident students was at Shaftesbury Hall, very near the Promenade in the centre of Cheltenham. Some of the lectures were held here, including Primary Education with our tutor Mr Bascombe. He would shake your hand when you met him, only realising too late that his hand was full of drawing pins, ready for putting up children's pictures!

My mention of Cheltenham's Promenade reminds me it is the only inland town in Britain that has one. Every other promenade is on the coast.

Our Theology tutor was Mr Robinson, brother of John Robinson, author of the controversial and then recently published "Honest to God".

On Sundays we would "do the rounds" of various churches, trying all the different denominations. I can remember hearing people speaking in tongues at the Pentecostal Church, and singing out with gusto at the Methodists. It was at this time that the idea of the Church of England and the Methodists joining together was mooted. It seemed to mean changes on both sides, and it didn't come to fruition. Looking back, I'm glad it didn't. I think nowadays we all respect and value our different ways of worship, and don't see the need for people to change to make everything uniform.

We were all studying Theology, and were very interested in all those different styles of worship, which was a frequent topic of conversation for us at mealtimes. Bob was a staunch Methodist and he and I went regularly to Monday evening Bible Studies at the Manse near the college.

In the holidays I carried on with my puppet shows which, as I said, continued to be a useful source of income.

<u>1971</u>

Decimal currency was introduced on 15 February (Stephen's birthday), and the Mersey Tunnel was opened. Education Secretary Margaret Thatcher was named "Milk Snatcher" as she ended the provision of daily free milk for children over seven.

In Florida, Walt Disney World opened ... which leads me to write a bit more about America!

One day, looking at the noticeboard in the entrance hall, I spotted an opportunity for fifteen students to go to Vermont on an exchange. It was to teach at a primary school there, and stay with a local family for five weeks. I spoke to Bob about it and we both decided to apply. No one could have been more delighted and surprised when our names were chosen. What an incredible adventure! I had never been abroad, not even to France, and neither had my parents, who didn't even possess a Passport.

We flew to JFK Airport, New York and were taken by bus 200 miles north to Burlington, Vermont. Bob England was placed with a gay couple, Bud and John, and I was placed with a family – Mike and Judy Tarre, and their two young daughters, Shari and Marci. We taught at Thayer Elementary School and made friends with several of the staff who invited us to meals in their homes.

There was an excellent, eccentric teacher called Martha Horrican. Quite a masculine woman, she wore suits with lapelled jackets each day. The children adored her, and would take their work up to her desk for her to mark or comment on. Sometimes she would say nothing at all but merely turn back one of her lapels. Underneath, hidden out of sight until it was revealed, was a badge. The badge was pinned so that it could only be seen when the lapel was turned back, which Ms Horrican did at certain appropriate times. It said "I think your story is very interesting – but stupid".

Mike and Judy were wonderful, generous hosts to me. The nature of Bob's hosts' relationship was never discussed or referred to. Bud was a white man, quite masculine, rugged, swarthy. John was a black man, handsome, smooth, slim, and very keen on the musicals, as I was. At the time, Jerry Herman's "Hello Dolly" was a continuing huge success on Broadway starring Carol Channing. John had the lp of the new all-black production with Pearl Bailey having replaced Carol.

I am one of the few people I know who can actually say they've been to Canada for the day! One Saturday, I took a train from Burlington to Montreal and went to a spectacular Disney on Ice show at a big Arena near the station.

The whole experience of living with an American family was just amazing, and Mike and Judy were very kind to me. I'd had a pretty sheltered upbringing even in British terms, so to go so far abroad to live and work was incredibly broadening for me. I had recently acquired a Super 8 cine camera, and I made a cine film of the five weeks, edited it and added a soundtrack of music and narration. This I showed to various family and friends, as well as at an American Evening at College. I started to make animated films, my first being Cinderella, which I was able to use as part of my submission of work towards my Art course. I fitted in well with the theological studies, and really enjoyed the discussions. However, although my animated films were well received by Mr Sayer the Art Tutor, I struggled quite a bit with graphic art, and I think now the idea of painting a picture is pretty much beyond me. Maybe that's because I have a very talented watercolourist for a husband, and my attempts would be a pale imitation! Each to their own.

<u>1972</u>

In America, news broke of President Nixon's involvement in the Watergate scandal. Who remembers that Mr Nixon was in fact a Quaker? Here Prime Minister Edward Heath declared a state of emergency as a result of the miners' strike.

I was back in the Hall of Residence for the final year at St Paul's, this time at Rosehill which was a mile out of town on the Evesham Rd, very near the famous racecourse. Not being able to afford a car, and never having learned to ride a bike, the mile-long walk to and from the town for lectures certainly kept me fit!

It was in this last year at college that we met "Auntie Grace".

A friend of Alun Williams, Bob Staley, invited our little group to Sunday tea with his parents at Thornbury near Sharpness. They were staunch Baptists and we went to their local Service after tea. We learned that Bob's aunt, Grace Ball, was the Minister at Foxcote Chapel, Andoversford. This was a tiny church out in the Cotswolds on the way to Bourton on the Water. Connections were made, and we were all invited to have tea with Auntie Grace at her house on the edge of Cheltenham.

This was a very significant moment. Alun Williams, Roger Wheelhouse, Roger Welshman, Bill Ives, Bob England and myself were to go on having these teas with Auntie Grace regularly for the next ten years. About once a month until the end of our course, we would all go out to see her and her son Brian who was quite significantly affected by Down's Syndrome, and greatly loved. Not owning a television, Auntie Grace was a fan of Jimmy Young on the radio, and his daily recipes. "What's the recipe today, Jim?" Her favourite was cheesie weesies, which she served hot, <u>every</u> time we went!

Once we had left college, we all returned three times a year when we would converge on Auntie Grace from our different parts of the country. We would have cheesie weesies, swap stories, and gather round the piano to lustily sing hymns. Brian's favourite, which was always included, was "Guide Me Oh!" as he would call it. Full title "Guide Me O Thou Great Redeemer".

You meet in life certain people who are a shining Light. Auntie Grace was the second in my life, the first being Father Moon at Millbrook in Southampton.

After a final and less pleasant teaching practice at a school in Gloucester (I can't remember the name of it), I went for several job interviews. I was offered a job at St Clements School in Bournemouth.

Looking back now, I can't believe that I declined the offer. I felt quite strongly that it wasn't right for me, and felt sure that the right offer would come along. What a risk to take. Anyway, I was later offered a job at Winton Junior, once again in Bournemouth. I can remember the headmaster, Mr Janda, asking me at my interview if I'd ever had any discipline problems during my teaching practices, and I said no, and him also asking me if I was always sober! Not sure if that would be asked nowadays.

I accepted the post at Winton and started there in the September of that year.

When we finally came to the end of our college course, we had a Leavers Service in the College Chapel and the

Principal, Mr Bradby, wished us luck in our careers wherever we might be starting. "After all," he said, "We can't all begin in Bournemouth!"

I moved back home to my parents in the summer, and then travelled north to Kendal in the Lake District to attend Roger and Sue's wedding. I went by train as far as Blackburn and stayed a couple of nights with my cousin Rosemary and her then husband Harvey. That way, I could go on a day return from Blackburn to Kendal, stay over again, and then return home the next day.

Soon it was time to travel to Bournemouth to start teaching in September. On my starting salary of £15 a week, there was still no way I could afford a car. Neither could I afford a flat. I took an attic bedsit near Cemetery Junction at £3.50 a week, and went by bus to the school each day. I soon made friends with several of my colleagues, including Trish who still lives nearby to us in Ferndown. We see her regularly, and she and her husband came to our Civil Partnership in 2007.

<u>1973</u>

On 1 January, the UK entered the European Union, the EEC as it was then I think, and as a result, VAT was applied to most goods and services.

Numerous IRA bombs were detonated in the UK, the Dalai Lama made his first visit here, and women were admitted to the London Stock Exchange for the first time.

Auntie Marjorie and Uncle Eric moved from Barnham up to Gatehouse of Fleet, near Kirkudbright in south west Scotland. This was to be their retirement home in a particularly beautiful but remote spot. My parents went by train from Southampton to Dumfries to visit them, Dumfries being by then the nearest station, with the railway "coast road" to Stranraer closed.

It wasn't until 1973 that I had saved enough money to buy a secondhand car – a 10 year old mini costing £150. I had been supplementing my teaching income by going out to do private tuition four nights a week, and had also carried on with my puppet shows which were a good earner. Was I a workaholic? Not really. It was just a case of "needs must".

My grandmother's second husband John Stimson died. She was to remain alone at her house in Alby Road for another six years, having seen out two husbands!

There were wonderful summer season shows in Bournemouth in those days, at The Pavilion, The Winter Gardens and the Pier Theatre. They would run for 16 weeks, and the two main ones were twice nightly Monday to Saturday, with different Sunday concerts. This year The Pavilion hosted The Black and White Minstrel Show. This would not be presented nowadays, but then it was just considered a top quality production with a great cast, a great orchestra, and great guest artistes.

One of the guest stars was top ventriloquist Neville King, and his son Shaun was placed in my class during the run.

Mr Janda our headmaster had seen how keen I was on showbusiness and thought the boy would do well in my class. What an opportunity that was.

I quickly made friends with his parents, and his father invited me to see him in the show whenever I wanted to go. I didn't have to have a ticket. I could just hang out backstage and watch from the wings. A dream come true. I had never been behind the scenes at a big theatre before. Now I could go about once a week to watch all the ways and means of putting on a big production.

I learned a lot which would stand me in good stead later on when Michael and I would become impresarios, putting on professional productions of our own at theatres all over the country – including, of course, the Bournemouth Pavilion.

There was a twelve piece orchestra with the Minstrels, but the Minstrels' singing was pre-recorded. A big reel-to-reel tape recorder played their voices in the wings, and the conductor in the pit had headphones on to keep the live instruments in time with the tape. One night the tape started off fine, but then began to play a little too slowly so all the voices were out of tune. They couldn't stop the show until the interval when they could retune the orchestra down a bit, so they struggled through, dancing around and smiling broadly while the audience winced at what they were hearing!

The most memorable night was one time when Neville's vent act wasn't going over well with a very cold, unreceptive audience. It was certainly falling on stony ground.

When he reached the end of his nine minute spot he said "You've been terrific, ladies and gentlemen. Good night everyone!" That was in the script, and was the same every time. This time, however, as he reached the cover of the wings where I and several others were standing, he added "and f*** the lot of you!" (He said it without any asterisks.) His radio mic was still on and these words were blasted out into the house over the loudspeakers. As luck would have it, the producer Robert Luff was "in" that night and, once he had calmed down, instructed Neville to apologise in the finale. Such is showbiz.

Something more that came from my association with Neville King was my being admitted to the actors' union Equity. He proposed me, and someone else from the show seconded, and I became a member. It turned out that they already had a Christopher Webb who was a stunt man - the guy who does all the dangerous things for a pittance, while the highly paid and cossetted "star" stands aside. I had to choose another name.

I can't really say why, but I quite quickly chose Derek Grant. I went through the phone book and chose a Christian name and a surname that seemed to go well together and sounded quite classy.

So I became Derek Grant professionally. Not only that, but Neville gave me his original design for his big vent puppet "Roddy the Rook".

I copied the design in every detail, producing an exact clone of his with lots of flowing ostrich feathers and a colourful jacket. I named mine Charlie the Crow, and thereby took my own show up a few notches - what with the Equity membership and the tips Neville gave me on performance technique.

I started to develop a one-hour show including vent-style routines with my new big Crow puppet, and other items featuring marionettes, glove and rod puppets. I moved from clubs and parties to performances in other Primary Schools which featured the one-hour show I'd developed, plus puppet making demonstrations and ideas for follow up work. The school holidays didn't coincide in the adjacent counties, so I could get bookings in Wiltshire and Hampshire schools.

Looking back, I can't imagine how I worked so hard. I was teaching full time at Winton Junior with all that entailed, I was still doing my private tuition several nights a week, and now I added numerous Charlie the Crow Shows. I was really "driven" I suppose, and determined to get somewhere, even though I didn't know where that was.

When I start to write later on about our life in the world of big showbusiness, I'll quote a few of the reviews our shows received. With that in mind, maybe now is the time to mention my favourite review of all regarding one of my own performances of my Charlie the Crow cabaret-style show at a working mens club in Southampton. When I'd finished, the Club Secretary paid me saying, "Well Mr Grant, now that I've seen your show, if anyone ever asks me what it's like, I'll be able to tell them."

<u>1974</u>

Britain suffered under a three day week, an attempt to save electricity during the long periods of strikes by coalminers. The Local Government Act changed many of our county boundaries and even moved Monmouthshire from England into Wales! (Not being too good on history, I think it might have originally been in Wales before being moved before. You may well know.)

Electric trains ran for the first time all the way from Euston to Glasgow.

At Holy Trinity Millbrook, Father Moon retired. He, his wife and daughter moved to Romsey, where he still preached occasionally at the Abbey.

Following on from my seasons a few years before at Debenhams Department Store, I approached the manager at Mayes, the store where my mother and I used to have coffee when I was growing up, and where I had been so taken with the young man who played the piano like Russ Conway. The deal was struck, and I did a run of five shows a day for a week in the school holidays in a specially constructed theatre they made for me on the top floor, very near the memorable coffee shop.

Fr Moon, his wife, and his daughter Mary came to see one of the shows at Mayes Department Store, and invited myself and my parents to visit them at their new house on the outskirts of Romsey, quite near the Plaza Theatre which Michael and I would play with our Bob Dylan Music Show fifty years later as part of our very last nationwide theatre tour.

Mary Moon was a little older, and also a teacher. She taught at Queensmount, a private girls' school at Charminster. We became friends and exchanged visits for meals together. Nothing was spoken but, looking back, she had not the slightest expectation of it becoming romantic any more than I did.

I had saved enough to buy a better car and also to move from the attic bedsit to a rented flat at Lower Parkstone. My college friend Alun Williams and I exchanged weekend visits regularly. He came to stay at Parkstone, and I went to stay with him in his house at Newton Abbot in Devon. I would meet his friends, one of whom was Connie Forman – a very dear soul, an eccentric, and a Quaker.

She loved poetry, among other things, and gave me a book of her own poems which included one "Meet Me at the Hasty Tasty". She wrote inside that she hoped one day to be able to meet me there. It was a small café near to the entrance to New Street Station in Birmingham. I'm afraid that was never to be. Connie has long since gone to her Maker, and the characterful little coffee shop she wrote about is now a branch of McDonalds. Says it all in a way, don't you think?

Alun had another Quaker friend (or should that be Friend?) called Leonard Bunnett, another complete eccentric, whom we would often visit on Sunday mornings when I was staying in Newton Abbot. In those days, I wasn't to know the significance Quakers would have in my life much later. But isn't that just the way of things?

I hadn't had a holiday since the last one with my parents in 1969, before I went away to college. This year, I took myself to north Wales and stayed in a self-catering studio at Bangor University. I was able to go from there to several of the narrow gauge railways I'd visited with my father, and also to Llandudno where I saw the two summer shows and made friends with Alex Munro who put on the open air show on the hillside below the Great Orme. I learned a lot from him in terms of performance, the "pacing" and structure of a show, and also the business side, as he was his own producer, hiring the venue and selling the tickets.

I was becoming a little more financially secure, and those were the golden days of showbusiness in Bournemouth. I could afford to see some of the greatest artistes of the day, who came to the town. A few of note included Maurice Chevalier, Andy Williams, Johnny Mathis, and Jack Benny. What an incredible comedian Jack Benny was. Rightly regarded as the best of his kind by other artistes, many of the top British comedians were in the audience to marvel at his technique, his control of the audience and his delivery. In those days, comedians, whether American or British, were just funny. Very funny. You couldn't tell what their politics were.

Jack Benny's persona was a man who was tight, cheap, stingy. To give you an example, Bob Monkhouse wrote a great line that Jack would use whenever he was in England.

"I'm staying over at a little place overlooking the Dorchester."

The stooge would ask "OVERLOOKING the Dorchester?"

"Yes. I figured, why pay the Dorchester prices, and overlook the DUMP where I'm staying?"

I discovered that my favourites The Bachelors were topping the bill for the summer season at Paignton, and decided to go and see them. Their show was presented twice nightly, six days a week, and my good friend Stephen Lee was performing matinees at the same theatre with the DaSilva Puppets along with his colleague, Peter Franklin.

Stephen has never been short of a quick, witty riposte, as I pointed out in my account of our visit to "Mame" with Ginger Rogers, and there was a memorable one during that particular season. There were several dressing rooms back stage. The Bachelors had the Number One room, plus another as their Lounge. The supporting cast were in the remaining ones, leaving Stephen and Peter to hang their stage clothes on a peg in the wings, along with their precious marionettes. There was a little boy who would sometimes watch the show from the wings. Stephen wondered if it was the son of one of The Bachelors. One time, he walked by only to spot the boy fiddling with the strings of one of the priceless puppets. Quick as a flash, Stephen loudly remarked "There's a word for the son of a bachelor, and you certainly live up to it".

<u>1975</u>

The Labour Party Conference voted against Britain continuing in membership of the EEC. There were snow showers in London in June – something that hadn't happened since 1761 – and inflation reached 24%!!

I struggled with my sexuality, which remained completely hidden and never expressed. Although homosexuality had been legalised between two men over 21 in private, any portrayal of such men on tv was rare, and then either high camp or tragic. John Inman, starring in "Are You Being Served" was highly entertaining, but it wouldn't have been a good idea to be like that in real life. "Queer-bashing" was common, and people like me were thought to bring such things upon ourselves if it ever happened.

Larry Grayson was hugely popular on tv. Teetering as I was, on the very edge of showbusiness, I was desperate to get in but didn't know how. I did have the chance to meet him backstage one time and found him personable and charming. He told me he thought Judy Garland was up above, pulling his strings so to speak, and guiding him through his performances.

Our Auntie Grace tea parties continued, with us all sharing our varied experiences of teaching in our different parts of the country.

I was starting to feel I would have to turn my back on my Christian faith if I were to pursue what seemed to be the right lifestyle for me.

It wasn't a choice to be the way I was. It was just a fact. The night terrors continued.

1976

The first commercial Concorde flight took off from Heathrow. The Queen opened the new National Exhibition Centre near Birmingham, and Anita Roddick opened her first Body Shop. Brotherhood of Man won the Eurovision Song Contest for Britain with "Save Your Kisses for Me" (Who said the Seventies were the decade when good taste died?) and the summer heatwave peaked at 97% Fahrenheit, the hottest place in the country being Cheltenham!

I was able to enjoy some really great shows in the West End and elsewhere. I saw people like Julie Andrews, Angela Lansbury and Tommy Steele in London, and nearer to home I could watch all the biggest British stars when they came to Bournemouth - Cilla Black, Mike Yarwood, Dick Emery, Val Doonican, Paul Daniels, Max Bygraves, Vera Lynn, and many more. Those were the golden days of seaside entertainment.

I've always enjoyed "light entertainment" and have taken great interest in the performance techniques of the biggest talents in that field, but my tastes can't really be categorised. I love the paintings of David Hockney, along with some of the Impressionists. I like to visit churches and cathedrals, and can appreciate a Bournemouth Symphony Orchestra concert as much as seeing Tommy Steele in pantomime, or a play by David Hare or Alan Ayckbourne.

Variety artistes, singers and comedians were quite a proportion of the people we presented once Michael and I became impresarios, and when we get to that part of my story, much of what I'll tell you about them is quite surprising!

Now, where was I?

1976 was the year of two more big changes for me.

Firstly, on one of my weekend visits, Alun told me he was taking a group of 11 year olds from his school to north Wales for a week in the summer holidays. Real holidays still being a little too expensive for either of us, it was a way to go somewhere free of charge (if you were willing to have twelve 11 year olds in tow all the time!) Alun explained that his colleague who was going to lead the trip with him had pulled out, and he had no one else to turn to for help. This conversation between us took place at the Pickwick Restaurant in Teignmouth, one of our favourite haunts. It didn't take me a moment to say "I'll come". I had nothing planned for August, I knew and loved North Wales, and always enjoyed Alun's company.

Alun had to approach his headmaster to ask if it would be all right for me to jointly lead the trip. Alun's headmaster contacted my headmaster, Mr Janda, for a reference and the deal was done! Alun had hired a house at Harlech and wc would go out on walks and rail trips each day, visiting Caernarfon Castle, Porthmadog, the Llechwedd Slate Caverns at Blaenau Festiniog, etc. etc. It was a very happy week, but hard work and a huge responsibility. This was also an extremely hot summer, the hottest on record. Rivers dried up, with river beds cracked like crazy paving. All this certainly didn't make the trip easier, but overall, it was very enjoyable and a way for Alun and me to have a holiday of sorts.

When we were back, Alun arranged a Welsh Evening at his school for all the parents to hear about our exploits. He and I told anecdotes and all of the children took part.

A little later in the year, we followed up with a day trip when we took the same group by train to Gunnislake, north of Plymouth.

Another memorable rail trip that year was to Norwich. British Rail started doing package holidays under the brand name Golden Rail. The return rail fare was included along with three nights in a good hotel. Bob England and I decided to go with Golden Rail to Norwich. Neither of us had been there, so it gave an opportunity to see the Cathedral, and we also took a day return to Great Yarmouth while we were there. We stayed at the three star Hotel Nelson, which was very good, and all at a bargain price!

Bob travelled across to London from Bristol, and I travelled up to Waterloo from Bournemouth, meeting at Liverpool Street to travel on the last leg together to Norwich.

In those days, there were compartments on trains, and on my journey up to Waterloo I found myself sharing with a couple from Southampton. We got chatting (as I always seem to do!) and they said their names were Ian and Doreen. They were both very interested in the theatre and they were on their way to London to see a matinee. Of course, we got on very well, swapping theatrical stories, and when we parted at Waterloo we exchanged names and numbers. I didn't think a great deal more about it, but as soon as I was home from the break in Norwich, the phone rang. It was Ian, inviting me to dinner, and to meet their resident friend Roye who was also a theatre devotee.

As I write in 2020, I have just been to see Ian and Doreen last week! Sadly, Roye passed away a few years ago, but Michael and I regularly exchange visits with Ian and Doreen to this day.

The second big change in 1976 was buying my first house. An advert appeared in the Bournemouth Echo for a new development of ten small terraced houses at Branksome. A mid terrace was £9450, and the two end ones were £9950. My father accompanied me to the building society to help with a mortgage application, standing as guarantor for the loan.

On a particular Saturday morning, the houses were going on sale at 9 am – first come, first served. I took a folding picnic chair and arrived at 6.30 to sit outside the estate agent's office. When I got there, six people were already in place, making me the seventh in the queue. Soon others appeared and the ten places were filled. As 9 o'clock drew near, people would drive up in their cars, count the ten of us, and then drive away again, shaking their heads in disappointment. Would things be so orderly now?

With the end terraces being too expensive at £500 more, I secured one of the mid-terraces, and by 9.30 had paid a £50 deposit. I was on my way to home ownership!

This was a great step in the right direction. No longer was I paying rent. Now my money was going towards an investment for the future – even though the mortgage payments were taking up more than half of my teaching salary, and the extra bills for rates, gas, electricity etc. took most of the rest. My private tuition and puppet shows became the only means of survival. The visits to big London shows would have to wait a while - "on hold".

<u>1977</u>

"Abigail's Party", Mike Leigh's suburban comedy opened in London starring his wife, Alison Steadman. The Queen's Silver Jubilee was celebrated with numerous events and an extra public holiday.

Jeremy Thorpe denied the attempted murder of male model Norman Scott, The Morecambe and Wise Christmas Show attracted an audience of 28 million, and inflation fell back to 16%.

This was the year of the last train to Wimborne. The station had closed in 1964 as part of the Beeching cuts, and the through route to Ringwood and Brockenhurst was lifted. A single line stub was retained from Poole through Broadstone to Wimborne and West Moors for freight. Now even this was to be taken away. British Rail ran four special "last trains" from Bournemouth Central to Wimborne and I rode on one of them. My father's cousins Ena and Cyril, Muriel, Charles, and Kathleen all lived in Wimborne. They came down to the station to greet us as we came in. When the train stopped, everyone explored the site during the ten minutes or so we had before the train returned to Bournemouth. People poured all over the tracks and many sidings, climbing up onto the remaining derelict platforms and taking photos. There was no question of "elf'n'safety". It was just assumed that everyone would be responsible for their own behaviour - which indeed we were.

Ena and Cyril's son is my cousin John. He is married to Wendy, and they have a son and daughter, Jonathan and Samantha. It was clear from our encounter at Wimborne Station that Jonathan, then aged 11 or 12, was going to be a keen rail enthusiast like many in our family. One of my relatives on my father's side had been a signalman, another a guard, and another a Station Master.

My next encounter with young Jonathan was when cousins Charles and Muriel brought him to see my "Charlie the Crow Show" at Wimborne's Allendale Centre. He was keen to help put everything away backstage after the show. At this time, after the closure at Wimborne, I had begun to be interested in tracing the remains of some of the other closed lines around Dorset. One of the most loved and mourned lines in the whole of the UK is the Somerset and Dorset, which ran from Bournemouth to Bath. Nicknamed by enthusiasts the "Swift and Delightful", it was more commonly known as the "Slow and Dirty". Once Dr Beeching had his way, it went down in history as the "Sabotaged and Defeated".

I took Jonathan out to Blandford Forum one Saturday to find the remains of the station there, and thus began many trips we would make, tracing the course of the whole line right up to Bath Green Park.

Bath Green Park is now a Sainsburys Supermarket, and Wimborne Station was demolished to make way for Wimborne Market. Now even that is to be closed! Is all this really progress?

Another relative on my father's side passed away, Aunt Lil (Matilda Eldridge). She'd lived at Horning Rd in Branksome with her sister Lucy who died in 1974, and we used to visit them every Christmas.

At Winton Junior, we had weekly visits from a peripatetic teacher, Marjorie Parkinson, and this being the Queen's Silver Jubilee, on that special occasion there were Union

Jack cakes for everyone instead of the regular rich tea biscuits.

I suppose, as a visitor Marjorie was a bit of an outsider, not being on the regular permanent staff. Looking back, I've always been something of an outsider myself, for obvious reasons. Did my father feel that way, with his interest in gypsies? Anyway, I was the only member of staff to really make friends with her.

Marjorie's husband was The Revd Keith Parkinson, vicar at St Augustine's, Cemetery Junction in Bournemouth. They both belonged to the William Temple Association, named after the famous Archbishop who did such a lot of work towards social justice. Once a month, evening meetings were held at the Lucullus Room at the Pavilion. There was a dinner and then an after-dinner speaker on some aspect of Theology. Marjorie and Keith invited me to go with them as their guest, and I later discovered that Mary Moon was a member as well. I went a couple of times with Marjorie and Keith, and another time with Mary. The William Temple Association will come back into my story in 2015.

Alun and I took more children to Wales in the August holidays. This year, we expanded our children's residential visits. I went with Alun on his trip from Decoy Primary in Devon to Harlech, and then two weeks later, he accompanied me on a Winton Junior week to the same place, where we repeated the itinerary one more time!

I contracted pneumonia.

The little house I'd bought didn't have central heating, just a couple of night storage heaters. One upstairs and one down. The front door opened into the little room downstairs, and there was a kitchen area at the back of the room behind a kind of screen. The stairs went up out of the room and upstairs there was one bedroom, a little box room and a tiny bathroom. If I'd shared the house with a cat, I wouldn't have been able to swing it.

Anyway, I was feeling a bit peeky one evening. It was a freezing cold night out, and I think I was running a slight temperature. Never being one to give in, I went out to the shops in any case, and caught quite a chill. The next thing I knew I was as ill as I've ever been. A raging fever, sweats and headaches, chest pains and breathlessness. The doctor confirmed pneumonia, which I'd more or less given to myself. If I'd nursed the slight temperature I had and taken care, I wouldn't have got so seriously ill.

I was off work for a month, and for most of the time went back to my parents in Southampton who looked after me famously.

I was only back to school for a few weeks when I fell down the stairs. Do you remember Mr Janda asking me if I was always sober? Well I was! Honest!

Anyway I broke my wrist, which had to be put in plaster. With it being my left wrist, and me being left-handed, I was completely unable to write. Now I was off work for

ANOTHER month! Thank goodness for state sponsored sick pay!

<u>1978</u>

The otter became a protected species, and Britain's first naturist beach opened near Hastings. Another more famous one at Brighton would open the following year.

Saturday night tv saw Larry Grayson taking over from Bruce Forsyth as host of The Generation Game, increasing the ratings to a new high of 21 million.

A memorable trip this year, without a party of 11 year olds in tow, was to Llandudno, again in Wales but further north. I already knew and liked Llandudno, having stayed there with my parents in 1964, and then visited again when I'd stayed at Bangor University.

This time, the holiday was organised by Wimborne cousin Ena. I went along with Bob England, and young cousins Jonathan and Samantha were also there. We set off from Wimborne by coach and stayed at a nice guest house on the front. Ena had arranged many day trips out and about, including to the Swallow Falls at Betws y Coed.

Unfortunately, I was attacked in the street. A man came up behind me as Bob and I were walking side by side on the High Street I didn't see him coming as he came from behind, and he struck me so hard that I fell forward onto the pavement, going down like a skittle. We hadn't been aware that he was behind us, and I don't know to this day why he attacked me.

Bob was amazingly quick thinking. Spotting the man going into a shop, he called the police from a nearby phone box and they arrived in three minutes to arrest the man. About six months later he was convicted of assault, and I was awarded £275 in compensation! The whole thing is a picture of very different times from those we live in today.

1979

Airey Neave was killed in the House of Commons car park by an Irish National Liberation Army bomb. Six weeks later, Margaret Thatcher became Britain's first female Prime Minister. Elton John performed in the Soviet Union, the first musician from the West to do so, and Sebastian Coe set a new world record for running a mile. Later in the year, Lord Mountbatten was killed by the IRA, and Bank Lending Rate was increased to 17%!

By this time, I had sold my tiny terrace at Branksome, and moved to a slightly larger and better terraced house at Corfe Mullen. This involved borrowing more and being committed to a larger mortgage – just, as it turned out, when interest rates rocketed. I don't know if you've ever tried paying a mortgage at 17% interest, but I don't recommend it.

The Summer Season at Bournemouth Winter Gardens that year was "The Cilla Black Show" with Cilla's special guest star Don Maclean, the quick-fire comedian of Crackerjack fame. It ran for 16 weeks twice nightly Monday to Saturday and I went to opening night. After Cilla's big opening number with the orchestra and large chorus of dancers, she introduced Don. She and he then proceeded to do around ten or twelve minutes of stand-up gags, banter between the two of them and various members of the audience sitting near the front. I was in awe of what they could do so effortlessly, bouncing off each other.

I thought with that being the first night, it was probably a bit of a one-off. However, when I returned to the show a few weeks later, the 12 minutes had become eight, certainly no less than that, and if anything was even more slick.

When Don Maclean worked for Michael and me three decades later, he confirmed what a great talent Cilla was, but he was disappointed not to have received a reply from her when he wrote sending condolences after her husband Bobby died.

My trips with Jonathan to the Somerset and Dorset railway locations continued. Cousins Charles and Muriel also brought him to my Charlie the Crow Show at The Tivoli Theatre in Wimborne. Again, he helped put everything away after the performance. As it turned out, mine was the last live show at the Tivoli before it closed. It had mainly been a cinema, with only occasional live shows. Terry Hall and Lennie the Lion were booked to appear, but the theatre closed and their show never took place.

18 years later, Michael and I appeared there on a Friday with our "Derek Grant's World of Puppets", and then presented

"The Bachelors Show" the following day, the Tivoli having reopened, brightened up and refurbished. This new incarnation of Wimborne's art deco theatre hosted top names like Cleo Laine and Johnny Dankworth, and our own Lesley Garrett Show. Manager Malcolm Angel told me the highest fee he'd paid for a star name was to Max Bygraves, who always sold out, and so was well worth the high price.

At Winton Junior School, our specialist music teacher retired. She had been running the choir, among other things, as well as playing the daily hymns on piano in assembly. Mr Janda asked me if I could take over these tasks.

Although I couldn't read music (you'll remember my lack of application to my poor mother's attempts to teach me), I could busk a tune fairly well – better than Les Dawson in any case. I readily agreed and enjoyed choosing and playing the daily hymns. Now, whereas the children had quietly filed into the assembly hall to the strains of Grieg or Mozart on piano, the best I could offer was "Chim Chim Cheree", or "How Do you Solve A Problem Like Maria?" which seemed to liven things up a little.

A couple of colleagues took it in turns to help run the choir and I introduced a repertoire of songs that were bright and breezy, and definitely entertaining!

I'm not sure that those members of staff who followed Phil Collins, Eric Clapton or other current favourites were particularly enamoured, but we had good numbers of both boys and girls wanting to join the choir and sing along to "A Spoonful of Sugar", etc. Who needs "The Ash Grove"?

Our school residential trips to Wales continued in the summer holidays. This time I went with Bob England on a trip from his primary school in Bristol. We stayed further south at Aberystwyth, using a group of rooms in the University. My main memory of that particular trip is that a chip of hot metal flew into a boy's eye. We were riding on the Vale of Rheidol steam railway to Devils Bridge, and the tiny fragment of metal was blown into his eye in the smoke from the engine. We had to take him to A&E, which involved careful and difficult logistics of caring for the other children as there were only the two of us.

Cousin Ena organised another coach holiday, this time to Margate. This was another place I had never visited. I went along and Roger Welshman joined me. We stayed in a guest house at Cliftonville and went on day trips around the local area, including to Canterbury Cathedral. In the evenings, Roger and I visited the summer season shows at the Winter Gardens and the Cliftonville Pavilion.

We saw Jim Davidson (not my favourite) in a big show at the Winter Gardens, and a smaller show at the smaller Cliftonville Pavilion featuring husband and wife comedy team Billy Whitaker and Mimi Law. Thirty years later, Michael and I were to present our own big Danny La Rue Show at Margate Winter Gardens, and we also met Mimi Law at the showbusiness retirement home Brinsworth House when we were at a garden party there.

<u>1980</u>

Robert Runcie became Archbishop of Canterbury, later going on to tell Anglicans that homosexuality should be seen as a handicap rather than a sin. The notion "glad to be gay", to which many of us subscribe, was born.

Great Aunt Lucy died. She was my father's aunt, a spinster living with her sister Lily in Branksome. My abiding memory of Aunt Lucy was a remark she nearly always made whenever we were there for family tea-parties. "Christopher doesn't look at the young ladies!"

Unemployment reached 2 million, there were riots at St Pauls in Bristol, and coal miners demanded a 37% pay rise.

Consett Steel Works were closed with the loss of 4500 jobs. Michael Foot became leader of the Labour Party, and the Queen became the first UK monarch to visit the Vatican.

The Yorkshire Ripper was at large, and John Lennon was murdered in New York.

My Grandmother Webb died. She had been living out her last days in a "home" just along the road from my parents' house in Shirley Ave. My father, as her loyal only son, visited her each day. I can remember her being terribly thin at the end, so much so that she made virtually no lump in the sheets as she lay in bed. Dad went to the mortuary on his own, and sat next to his mother's body in the Chapel of Rest. My father was a deep, thoughtful man who didn't express his feelings, inhibited as men generally were back then.

The funeral was held in Bournemouth, and afterwards we went to the Carlton Hotel on the East Cliff for the wake.

Uncle Eric died. This was the second funeral of the year. I have never witnessed grief such as that shown by Auntie Marjorie. It was terribly moving to see her in such extreme distress. Uncle Eric had been a man who was the life and soul of the party, but in later years had suffered with Parkinsons Disease, a disease that would go on to take my brother Peter 40 years later.

After the death of her husband, Auntie Marjorie moved back down south, to London in fact, where she bought a house at Ealing in the parallel road to where her daughter, my cousin Jennifer lives. This enabled Auntie Marjorie to go into town quite often for matinees. She and I could compare notes on plays and musicals, but not on opera which was her taste not mine.

This was also the year of my first "encounter" - and I had got to the age of 29! I'm afraid I can't now remember the young man's name, except to say that he was two or three years older than me, very pleasant, very good looking, and we only met the once. The event was completely hidden and clandestine obviously, as the whole culture of the times was that we should be thoroughly ashamed of ourselves.

I can still remember now, as I write in 2020, comments made over the years such as Great Aunt Lucy's oft-repeated observation. Remarks such as that had always struck terror in my heart − firstly that I would not be able to change, and secondly that I must never be found out. How could I not be found out, however, when I knew I never would look at young ladies in the way I was expected to?

Bob England and I went again to America, and revisited Mike and Judy Tarre. They had moved from Vermont to Chappaqua near New York. We stayed with them for a few days and then went by train to Washington where we stayed in a Best Western Hotel and saw the sights − the White House, the Lincoln Memorial etc. Finally, we went on to Philadelphia before flying home.

Neither of us being able to afford tickets to any Broadway shows, Mike got tickets for Bob and me to see The Pyramid Game being recorded at a tv studio in Downtown Manhatten. Dick Clark was the host, and we discovered they recorded five episodes in a row, one after the other, in a marathon presentation. These would then be shown daily on national television "coast to coast" as they said, Monday to Friday. The guest star for this particular week was Mickey Rooney. He would be there for all the five days, but of course it was all recorded in the one session.

After the first 25 minute episode was completed, the one for Monday, Mickey said he would answer audience questions while the crew were getting ready for taping the next one. One lady asked what his favourite film was. A man asked who was his favourite co-star. He answered quite pleasantly. Then he pointed to a lady near us whose hand had been stretched high in the air for a long time. "Yes!" he said. "The lady in the fourth row."

She looked like she was going to faint as she realised she was going to be speaking to her all-time idol.

"Mickey," she stammered. "You've always been my top favourite. I've seen all your films countless times, and I just want you to know I love you, Mickey."

"That's not a question. That's a statement," he snapped. "Next!"

When everyone was ready, filming began for the next episode. The one that would go out on the Tuesday.

Dick Clark stepped forward into the spotlight, his teeth gleaming in a fixed smile. "I'm delighted to say that our guest star today, once again, is the great Mickey Rooney."

Mickey ran out from behind the pyramid again, as Dick continued "It's great to have you with us again, Mickey. Since you were on yesterday, we've been inundated with calls from people saying it's great to see you on television again."

The "yesterday" he was referring to was just half an hour before, and no one had left the set in between the episodes. Nothing had yet been shown on air.

I'm sure I'll say again before I finish this book, "That's showbiz!"

When the second episode was completed, we decided to call it a day. There was no need to watch the other three episodes, as by then we had a pretty fair idea what they'd be like.

We stepped out again into the daylight of Manhatten and visited the World Trade Centre, going to the top in a lift. What an incredible view. Ten years earlier, Bob and I had been to the top of the Empire State Building, and I still have the souvenir dish I bought then. Little did we know that 20 years later, the World Trade Centre would be completely destroyed in an Islamist terrorist attack, with numerous people murdered.

Later that year Bob married Denise in a ceremony at Dover, Denise's home town. I wasn't able to go as I was taken ill just before the big day. I'd already booked the hotel, and it was such a pity to miss the big event.

Bob and Denise are still staunch Methodists, and Michael and I still see them regularly, as they now live at Seaton, not too far away.

Holidays on a more basic and regular level around this time had come to consist of home exchanges with Roger and Sue. Roger had left teaching and they were living at Bromsgrove where Roger was now Revd Roger and was the Baptist Minister. The exchange worked well. They really enjoyed using my house for a week or two near Bournemouth, Poole and the Purbecks, while I greatly enjoyed a Midlands Railrover based at their house.

86

In those days, the rover ticket was £7 for the week. For £1 a day you could "rove" by rail wherever you liked throughout an enormous area bounded by places like Shrewsbury, Stafford, Derby, Stratford upon Avon and Worcester, all centred on Birmingham New Street Station from where all the lines radiated, including the one going south west to Bromsgrove.

Our dear friend and shining light, Grace Ball "Auntie Grace" passed away. She died peacefully in her sleep in her own tiny front room. Her son, Brian wasn't able to understand what had happened to his mother, and stayed with her a long time until the death was discovered. I wasn't able to go to the funeral, working at Winton Junior School in Bournemouth, but was greatly saddened by her passing. The end of an era.

Brian Ball was moved to a "home" where he survived a few more months. I'm very glad Roger Welshman and I visited him there. Auntie Grace's love for him had been so strong and complete, that he just couldn't carry on without her. I don't think he ever understood what had happened.

My good friend Steve Lee left the DaSilva Puppet Company and set up a new enterprise with his friend and colleague Peter Franklin. They called it The Puppeteers' Company, and quickly became very successful, performing around 350 shows in schools each year. The sheer artistry of their puppets and settings set them apart from others, and this, combined with the sparkling wit of their after-show demonstrations, ensured the teaching staff loved them and booked them again and again.

1980 was also the year of my filming with cousin Jonathan. As I said before, we were both keen on the history of the now-closed Somerset and Dorset Railway, and this was the year we set about creating a Super 8 film of what remained. Quite a few Saturdays were spent on day trips to Blandford Forum, Sturminster Newton, Shepton Mallet, Wincanton, Radstock etc. and we finally filmed the last sequence in Bath. I edited the whole production, adding sound track and narration. The film is still here in its box on the shelf in my study, together with several railway films my father and I made. On my "to do" list is to have them converted into dvds, which I've promised myself I'll do this year before I'm 70.

<u>1981</u>

A parcel bomb was intercepted, addressed to Margaret Thatcher who had been called by some the most unpopular Prime Minister since the war. She certainly divided opinion, with many others seeing her as our saviour.

Several centrist Labour MPs formed the Social Democrat Party and entered an Alliance with the Liberals. Enoch Powell warned of "racial civil war", and there were extensive riots in most major cities. Moira Stuart became Britain's first black newsreader, and Arthur Scargill became leader of the National Union of Mineworkers.

The Queen opened the Humber Bridge, and Prince Charles married Lady Diana Spencer.

At Winton Junior School, we would have an annual Summer Fair, and an annual Sports Day. For the Summer Fair, I would teach some of the older children to make puppets and perform with them as an attraction during the afternoon. For the Sports Day, with sport not being my thing, Mr Janda the headmaster appointed me as commentator. This was right up my street. With a microphone in my hand and big loudspeakers out on the field, I introduced each race, announced the winners, and generally hosted the whole thing.

Mr Janda's wife, Phyllis, was no more interested in the races than I was, and each year she would sit with me at my table chattering away while I was having to think about what to say next and keep the whole thing going. She, like me, loved nice hotels, and the afternoon would go something like this.

I would turn on the mic to say "Could we have the contestants for the 100 yards now, please? All 100 yards contestants over to Mrs Mitchell now."

As soon as I turned the mic off, she'd say "We're at the Imperial again next weekend. It's the only place to stay in Torquay. They do everything so well, and if you have one of the Premier Rooms, you get the best table in the restaurant and, of course, the best sea view."

I remember once during a Sports Day, telling her about my interest in preserved railways. "Oh yes," she said. "The romance of steam!"

She turned to me and continued "Do you find steam trains romantic?" and without thinking I just said "yes".

"I thought so," she agreed. "I suppose you have to get some romance somehow into your life".

Wimborne bypass opened. The traffic had become horrendous, passing through the town on the way to the resorts in Devon and Cornwall. I always connect the opening of the bypass with the death of cousin Charles (Charlie) as I drove for the first time along the new road on my way to see his wife Muriel when I heard of his death from Wendy.

Charles Stout had been headmaster at St James School, Gaunts Common, just to the north of Wimborne. The first encounter that I can remember with Charlie and Muriel was when I was about 11 or 12. We went to the school when they were celebrating their wedding anniversary (maybe their 25th) and they held a big party in the school hall.

My father was asked to play the saxophone, and my mother the piano, and Charles took me out by myself into his study during the celebrations, where he proudly showed me his cane. He didn't offer a demonstration, and I don't know to this day whether one would have been given if I'd asked. The viewing of the cane was the only apparent reason for the visit to his study, and we then returned to the main gathering in the hall. How we remember these things from childhood, don't we?

<u>1982</u>

The Sun newspaper reached four million daily sales, and unemployment reached three million, the highest level since the war. Mrs Thatcher continued to divide the nation.

The lowest ever UK temperature was recorded at minus 27 degrees Centigrade at Braemar in Scotland. Two notable visitors to the UK were Pope John Paul II and USA President Ronald Reagan.

The Falklands War began after Argentina invaded the Falkland Islands, and the IRA detonated two bombs in London killing and maiming 55 people. The UK telegram service ceased, and Channel Four was launched.

Mrs Thatcher's government brought into law "Section 28". This banned what was described as the "promotion" of homosexuality in schools or what she called "pretended family relationships". The idea was that if teenagers heard about such a thing, they might want to try it. No one seemed to realise that you are as you are. We are all as the Good Lord made us.

Pretended family relationships? I have never been a political activist, but I so much admired the peaceful protesters with their banners which read "We are NOT pretending!"

Who could have thought that just fifteen years later Michael and I would be married?

Our headmaster, Mr Janda retired. There was a real outpouring of gratitude and warmth from the parents, with huge numbers of messages, letters, cards and presents. Mr Janda had the ability to appoint talented and capable staff who could give his school a good name. We ran a very tight ship, as they say, but the children felt secure and thoroughly enjoyed learning. We were known as "the happiest school in Bournemouth".

There was an interview process and a new head teacher, Mrs Munday, was eventually appointed to succeed him. This brought about great change!

Stage Four:
London University and Love.

In which I "find myself" in London, move back to Dorset and meet my true love. I leave teaching and become a mail order businessman.

<u>1983</u>

Unemployment reached 3.25 million, Margaret Thatcher went on to achieve another landslide victory in the Election, and Michael Foot resigned as Labour Leader. Saga Magazine was launched, along with the first Dyson vacuum cleaner and breakfast tv.

David Frost called breakfast television "the last great frontier of broadcasting". Little did he know!

The £1 coin replaced the £1 note. Seatbelts became compulsory in cars. CDs began to replace vinyl lps.

Things carried on under a new, very different regime at Winton Junior School, with the established staff struggling somewhat to understand the aims and objectives of the new headmistress.

With the ongoing lack of a true music specialist, I continued to run the choir, producing end of term concerts and taking part in county-wide contests. While other schools were singing "All Things Bright and Beautiful" or the ubiquitous "Lord of the Dance", we offered songs from the shows! Cheesy or what?

One day at school, our new headmistress Mrs Munday asked to see me. She said there was an opportunity for someone from the staff to be seconded to London University for a year to train for possible headship, and she wanted to offer it to me. She said I could think about it and let her know in due course. Never being one to beat about the bush, and often being compared to a bull in a china shop, I said right away, "I can tell you now!"

The deal was done, and in the September, instead of starting the new term with a new class at Winton Junior, I started at London University Institute of Education.

During the summer, before going away to London, I went to stay on the Isle of Wight with my school friend Brian Hinton. At the time, Brian was Librarian at Freshwater Library. Brian is a gifted poet and has had a lot of success with his writing. Nowadays, he is the Curator of Dimbola Art Gallery.

We went to see Cilla Black in her summer show at Sandown Pavilion and Brian wrote a poem about the experience, saying that Cilla entered the stage like a double decker bus.

I'm not sure I would have chosen that metaphor. Whilst dividing opinion on her singing, no one could deny that she had great stage presence. She walked on with confidence and authority, immediately engaging with the audience in her persuasive patter. Hugely entertaining.

Everyone remembers "Step Inside Love", "Anyone Who Had a Heart", "You're my World", and of course "Alfie", my favourite of her songs. Some will know that she only agreed to record it if composer Burt Bacharach was actually present. This was arranged and they did take after take. Eventually Cilla asked him what he was looking for.

"For that little bit of extra magic".

"I think you'll find that in take five."

This was certainly the case, as her huge success with the single went on to prove. A track that's still constantly played today.

Dionne Warwick had the hit with the song in America, and used to include disparaging remarks about Cilla's version in her act. Not very professional, to my mind.

When autumn came, I went away to London, having let my house in Corfe Mullen through managing agents. I decided to live in Hall again, like I'd done at St Paul's 15 years before. There was a cafeteria in the basement in Hall, and all the new students congregated there for the first evening meal. I had to dive in and attempt to get to know somebody at least! Quite a daunting prospect as most of the intake were 18 and 19 year olds and I was almost thirty three!

Once again, like my time at King Edward VI School and then at Cheltenham, it was an all-male environment.

In the event, I managed to gel with some of the foreign students who were also a little bit outsiders like I was. I made friends with Randall, a Canadian studying law, a handsome Greek called Stelios (who subsequently invited me to his wedding in Athens!), Frank, an American studying theatre arts, and Sebastian, a stunning guy from Zimbabwe who was so very charming. Only Sebastian was on my own course. All the others were on different ones which helped to broaden the whole thing.

Everyone on my course was an established teacher. Some were already heads, and most were hoping to get headships. We went altogether to thirty different schools in the London area, spending half a day observing in each, and then writing up our experiences. In lectures and seminars we would compare notes and express candid opinions on what we'd seen.

The time in London was when I finally found myself. I could fulfil my love of theatre very easily. Imagine living in walking distance of the West End and being able to see as many plays and shows as I wanted, all at student rates!

But that wasn't all. I knew I was 100% gay. Now I could express it. I will put this decorously and just say that it was during my time in London that I was finally able to "celebrate" my sexuality!

All that took place in a parallel existence to my life in the University, however. There, I continued to hide my identity from my fellow teachers and lecturers – even my friends in

Hall. Nothing was ever said or revealed. Not the best thing for my mental wellbeing.

If only I'd been "normal" I could have found a young lady, and then I could have happily told everyone about her. Surely my lifestyle was "a disgrace to anyone living"?

I saw many amazing plays. Rupert Everett in "Another Country", Maggie Smith in "Interpreters", Penelope Keith in "Hay Fever", and many more, plus West End musicals including "Guys and Dolls", "West Side Story" and fringe events including gay plays and late-night cabarets. Some could be spoken about. Some could not. The night terrors continued.

<u>1984</u>

The Footsie 100 Index was created, there were more miners' strikes, and in the schools, GCSEs replaced O Levels.

Torville and Dean won gold medals at the Winter Olympics and the Church of England agreed to the Ordination of women as Deacons, but not as full priests.

Tommy Cooper died on stage at Her Majesty's Theatre at the age of 63 during a live broadcast. Other notable deaths this year included Diana Dors, John Betjeman, Eric Morecambe and Richard Burton.

The story used to be told of Tommy Cooper in the line-up after the Royal Variety Performance one year. When the Queen came along, you weren't supposed to say anything except to briefly reply if SHE spoke to YOU. I don't know if it's apochryphal or not, but Tommy is supposed to have cheekily piped up, saying "Excuse me your majesty, but could I just ask you – are you keen on football?"

"Well not particularly, no."

"Oh! Well in that case, could I have your Cup Final tickets?"

I was having the time of my life in London. I made a couple of friends outside Uni, one being Tony Phillimore. He was a guy of about my age, living in Arnos Grove, Southgate with his partner Barry. Tony and I had a completely platonic friendship, going to the theatre together numerous times. Later, when I left London University to go back to Dorset, I went to stay with him many times, until he found a new love and moved away to France.

During my year in London, Tony and I also travelled together to Portsmouth to see Cilla Black at the Kings Theatre there. We queued to meet her signing her book after the show, and she told us that she was soon starting two new television series, Blind Date and Surprise Surprise.

Just after that, there was an advert in the Evening Standard for free tickets to television shows at London Weekend TV on the South Bank. You could just make a general application. It didn't say what the shows would be.

Full of enthusiasm, I applied and soon became the lucky recipient of two free tickets to Surprise Surprise! This was a much better experience than Bob England and I had had in

New York with Mickey Rooney. Cilla herself did her own "warm up".

Most tv shows employ an unknown comedian to get the audience going before the star appears. This way the star entertainer has a much easier time and goes down well with the crowd. That's then the only bit that's shown on the screen. (Some will know that Peter Kay began by being the warm up man for Parkinson, before finding fame himself.)

Anyway, I was so impressed that Cilla undertook this task herself. She spent around 25 minutes chatting and entertaining, something I'd seen her do five years earlier with Don Maclean at Bournemouth Winter Gardens. The Surprise Surprise show involved sequences with audience members in reunions with long lost friends or family and here Cilla had well and truly done her homework. She rattled off all sorts of facts about each person she interviewed without any cue cards or autocue. Clearly a true pro, and someone with a genuine interest in what she was doing.

How could I not mention that 1984 was the year of The Bachelors' acrimonious split? During a much-publicised court case at the Old Bailey, John Stokes left the group and was replaced by Peter Phipps. This was just before their already agreed summer season for Bernard Delfont at the Congress Theatre Eastbourne, the largest theatre on the south coast.

Roger Welshman and I, both being fans, went to stay in Eastbourne to see "The New Bachelors" in a big production with orchestra, chorus and guest stars. The adverse publicity of the split had taken its toll. With John Stokes no longer appearing, Con and Dec now sang alongside Peter, a new unknown third member. We went into the box office to book for the following day. "Would you like stalls or circle?" we were asked.

"Stalls, please."

"Would you like to sit in the very front row?"

"Well ... er ... yes ... that would be lovely."

"Whereabouts in the front row would you like to sit?"

Are you getting the impression that the house was sparse to say the least?

John Stokes will reappear in my story.

My other trip in 1984 was to Amsterdam. After Eastbourne with Roger, I took advantage of the last few weeks of my student discount and went to Amsterdam where I visited all the hot spots, to put it mildly.

Finally, we come to the most important event of 1984. Just before I left London, my brother Peter came to visit me. He said he had a proposal to make. I couldn't imagine what it would be, and was amazed when he said he wanted to leave teaching and start a business. I'm sure Cilla would have said "Surprise Surprise" once again if she'd only known!

Peter said I was the only person he could consider running a business with. The only thing needed was an idea.

At that time, I was intending to go back to teaching at Winton Junior School. I hadn't considered leaving the profession. Nevertheless, it was true that I certainly felt differently about life in general now I'd "come out", if only to myself. Teaching was becoming very different too. There were computers on the horizon, and in Peter's eyes schools were gradually putting the children in charge! He could see the writing on the wall, he said, and if we stayed more than a couple more years we'd be taken away in a van by the men in the white coats.

Unbelievably, just at that time I'd been pondering an idea. I'd had the notion that to create something new, you needed to combine two existing things that were separately established but hadn't been combined before. Disco music was all the rage, seen to be "cool" by the young. Parents, and grandparents in particular, were increasingly concerned that children were no longer being taught the basics, spelling, times tables.

I had the idea of something we would go on to call "Tables Disco". Peter was a musician, a keyboard player, and he moonlighted several nights a week, playing keyboard in clubs and hotels around the Southampton area. We recorded all the tables from 2s to 12s to music Peter created, and with my dulcet tones reciting them all to a disco-beat! This made a kind of an lp or album for primary children and their parents to make learning multiplication tables quick, easy and fun. Not only did we provide each one recited a couple of times, we also provided test tracks where the answer wasn't given and you had to call out the right number in the gaps. We put the whole thing on to a cassette tape and started off by having 500 copies made. We sent a press release out to everyone we could think of, telling all about what we'd done and why we'd done it!

To cut a long story short, it was a great success. The Daily Telegraph asked for a review copy for their Education Editor. When he wrote that our tape "succeeded beyond all expectation", we were on radio and tv, in numerous women's magazines, and several other national newspapers. It was all very exciting, but VERY hard work. However, we were both on our way to leaving teaching and becoming businessmen. That would take a few more years, with many ups and downs along the way. A good few very expensive lessons were about to be learned!

My brother Peter was a very fine man, and quite unusual. One of his greatest pleasures, he told me, was knowing that no one else could ever know what he was thinking!

To give you an example of the way his mind worked, I'll tell the story of the time Michael and I went to Towles Restaurant in the New Forest with our friends David and William. On the way there, David told us that there would be a pianist, and she always played requests. He asked me what I would choose if given the opportunity. Straight away I said "Oh What A Beautiful Morning" from "Oklahoma!"

When we arrived at the restaurant, we walked in to find the pianist playing "Oh What A Beautiful Morning" from "Oklahoma!"

Don't you think that's amazing?

When I next saw my brother, I told him the story and said "Isn't that the most amazing coincidence?"

"It's not a coincidence at all", Peter replied.

"Why ever not?"

"Because," he said, "I can assure you that at that very moment there were millions of pianists all over the world who were NOT playing Oh What A Beautiful Morning".

That was my brother.

<u>1985</u>

The first mobile phone calls were made in the UK. (Just look at us now!), East Enders was launched, and Manchester United won the FA Cup for the sixth time. Sadly, the first death from AIDS was recorded, and Wilfrid Brambell, famous as Steptoe, died. I had only just seen him in an excellent production of Arnold Ridley's "The Ghost Train" in the West End.

Other showbusiness deaths included comedian and entertainer Dickie Henderson, whom I had met with Neville King a decade before, and first lady of Crossroads, Noele Gordon. Crossroads will return to my story later. Jilly

Cooper's raunchy novel "Riders" was published, and I wouldn't have guessed that I would go on to visit Jilly at her house in the Cotswolds in the years to come.

I moved house again. Corfe Mullen was becoming a little too far away from where I spent a lot of my time. I saw a lot of the Wimborne cousins, and of course travelled daily to Bournemouth to go to work, and to the theatre.

I managed to sell the terraced house at Corfe Mullen and buy a small detached house on quite a nice, well-established estate at Colehill, a suburb of Wimborne up the hill a bit to the north. This would be the house I would share with the only love of my life, whom I would meet the following year. For the moment, though, following my "finding myself" in London, I had a couple of proper boyfriends, each for a few months. The first, like me, had a cabaret act and has gone on to work for a leading pantomime company. The second met my friends Ian, Doreen and Roye. That's about all I can say about him!

<u>1986</u>

Unemployment reached almost 15% of the workforce. The UK and France announced the construction of the Channel Tunnel, and Prince Andrew married Sarah Ferguson. The Independent newspaper was born, and the M25 motorway was completed. Hilda Baker (she knows yer know), Dame Anna Neagle and Cary Grant all passed away. I had seen Anna Neagle in a very good revival of My Fair Lady with

Tony Britton as Professor Higgins, being too young to have seen Julie Andrews and Rex Harrison in the original.

After two years, the business my brother Peter and I were running had expanded enough for him to leave teaching and work on Tables Disco full time. I carried on at Winton Junior, but was keen to join him. The financial risks were huge, however, and I had a big mortgage to pay. By this time, we'd called the business Webucational (Peter's idea) and re-recorded the disco tables tape, updating it and improving the quality. We'd also produced some more recordings featuring fun ways to learn spelling, the alphabet, telling the time, etc. which gave us quite a selection of educational tapes to sell.

My brother Peter and I were getting more and more communicative, with business matters and everything. It seemed impossible to carry on with the kind of double life I was leading, and so after much soul searching, I decided to "come out" to him, the first time I'd attempted this with anyone. It went quite well, with him saying it wouldn't make any difference to our business or our relationship, the implication being that for many people being gay WOULD make a difference to everything.

I continued to have a number of "one-night-stands", but was growing tired of the chase. I decided to place a personal ad in Gay Times looking for something more. In those days, you got replies by post after quite a delay. As it turned out, this was to be the biggest change of my life. I had five replies and met them all. There wasn't really any connection with the first four, but being brought up to be polite, I spent a good hour or so with each one, chatting and comparing notes.

I had a reply from Michael Loughlin, who said he had moved to Bournemouth and was working in catering. He said he wasn't looking for a "fling", but someone to share his life. He also said he was often too trusting and could be easily hurt. What an admission to make as an opening gambit.

We arranged to meet at 7pm outside Debenhams in Bournemouth Square on a particular evening. We were both there on time, and quickly recognised each other from what we'd both written. We walked down through the gardens to the pier and along the front all the way to Boscombe talking all the time. Michael was most revealing and so was I. When we got back to the pier, we then walked west all the way to Alum Chine, still talking.

We finally parted and the next day Michael rang to say he wanted to see me again. To be honest, I hadn't really expected that. I'd had it drummed into me by my family and society in general that gay men weren't loved. There was no question of people like that having any kind of a real relationship.

Michael felt differently.

Definitely, more than anything else in my life, "Meant to be!"

Once again, I need to cut a long story short. Michael came several times to my small house at Colehill, and I went several times to his bedsit at Charminster. The visits became more frequent, then daily. After just a couple of months, we knew we wanted to be together. Michael gave notice to his landlord and moved in with me. I had always lived alone and liked my own company. In a way, I'd been something of an only child as Peter was almost 11 years older than me. For example, when I was eight, he was nineteen. This made me pretty much an only child, as you can surely understand.

It was a huge adjustment for me to have someone there all the time. Michael managed to get a catering job in Wimborne at Flight Refuelling and I continued at Winton Junior. However, it wasn't easy, to say the least, to come out to my colleagues which naturally I wanted to do. Conversation in the staffroom invariably consisted of chat about husbands. I really didn't see why I shouldn't mention my new life with Michael. To give you an idea of the response, most colleagues had little to say on the matter (mercifully!) but I got verbal abuse from one member of staff, who had himself had numerous extramarital affairs behind his long-suffering wife's back.

Once it became clear that we were going to be an item, the problem arose as to how to "come out" to everyone else generally.

I was at my brother's house and I managed to say to my sister-in-law Barbara that I thought I'd found the right person. "What's her name?" she asked.

When I said it wasn't a she but a he, there was concern over the fact that Auntie Marjorie was coming to lunch and what would she think.

I had to tell my parents. I spoke to my father first. I braced myself to talk to the man who had told me in my teens that homosexuals were the scum of the earth. The conversation was fairly brief, stilted and he offered to tell my mother, which was very good of him as he pointed out how upset she would be.

The outcome was that nothing would change their love for me, but they didn't want to meet Michael. They just couldn't face that. I was reduced to begging. I said "I beg you to meet him", which was particularly humiliating, but miraculously they eventually agreed.

As it turned out, they got on very well with Michael, and we started regular visits for Sunday teas. My mother liked cakes more than any other food, and her way of hospitality for everyone was tea, scones, cream buns, and Victoria sponge! Michael and I worked hard to build bridges, but whenever he met any of my parents' associates, he was introduced as my lodger. I suppose we had to be thankful for small mercies.

I got on well with Michael's parents also. His father Tony was quite a military kind of man who would march around barking instructions at his wife. Michael's mother Gina was devout, studying the Bible daily, which led her to view her son's relationship with me as sinful, rather than loving. One time, she and I were doing the washing up together in the kitchen of their flat on the West Cliff in Bournemouth. She suddenly said, "I can see you are sincere, but you must know how I feel".

Things progressed slowly, and we did eventually manage to arrange a meeting between our respective parents at our house in Colehill. My mother by then was in a wheelchair, suffering from arthritis, and Michael's mother was very caring and attentive to her. It was clear the two sets of parents would get on really well, and Michael's parents even invited mine to stay with them. This proved to be a step too far and no one was able to take things any further. It was very painful for all concerned, not the least for the two of us who had caused all the trouble.

In the autumn of 1986, as an indication of the way Michael and I would change each other and grow, I went to two rather different concerts in Bournemouth. Michael's all-time favourite was, and still is, Bob Dylan. We saw him at Wembley Arena along with Tom Petty and the Heartbreakers. Quite a change from Cilla Black!

We also saw Joan Armatrading at the Bournemouth International Centre. I've come to appreciate both these artistes over the years. We've seen them both again on several occasions and I've got quite a few tracks by each of them on my Ipod, tracks I greatly enjoy. Strangely, Michael hasn't got ANY by Cilla!

Things do go both ways, though, and I introduced Michael to all-time great artistes like Tony Bennett, Judy Garland, Andy Williams, Peggy Lee, Ella Fitzgerald and many more who now feature on his regular playlists, along with lots of songs from the films and shows we both like. (Can you believe Dame Judi Dench has never seen The Wizard of Oz, while the rest of us have all seen it at least fifty times?)

1987

Terry Waite was taken hostage in Beirut, where he would remain captive until 1991. The Church of England agreed to the full ordination of women.

Christies sold one of Van Gogh's "Sunflowers" for £24.75 million, and British Rail changed the name of second class to standard class. In the General Election, Margaret Thatcher won a third term with another huge majority of over 100, and Jeffrey Archer won a libel case against the Daily Star which had alleged he was involved in vice rings. He would go on to be imprisoned for perjury in 2001.

In a sign of times to come, customs officers seized £50 million worth of cocaine, and one person a day was now dying of AIDS. Notable deaths included actress Hermione Gingold, and cellist Jacqueline du Pre.

One of the greatest losses I had suffered so far was my Christian faith. I was "high church" through and through. I loved the liturgy of the Book of Common Prayer, and the Sung Eucharist. All this I'd left behind due to my sexuality, not believing people like me were welcome at the Lord's

Table. It was very painful, though, and a real gap that was crying out to be filled.

Michael had been brought up as a Baptist. Whereas I'd been baptised as an infant, and then confirmed by the Bishop of Winchester in my late teens, Michael had been baptised as an adult by total immersion. He had left the church for the same reason as I had, and when we met, had just started a dalliance with the Quakers. There was a Meeting House in Bournemouth, and another in Poole and he was keen for me to go with him. Could this be something we could do together?

I found the silent worship unhelpful to say the least, and I also didn't see the Meeting as Christian.

Michael was particularly keen for us to worship together somewhere, and so we set out on a journey around the churches of Wimborne. We tried Methodist, Baptist, C of E, etc. even Pentecostalist, but everywhere were met with the same thing. Although people were polite, you could see they were struggling to understand who we were. Why were two men together? Were they brothers? Had they left their wives at home?

In light of this, we just couldn't settle anywhere. We did manage to go to the Parish Church in Colehill for a while, even going to a Bible Study at the vicarage one time and a prayer meeting at a parishioner's home. That was quite memorable! The young lady leading it became so virtually aroused as she prayed that she was nearly to orgasm by the time she'd finished. Her young husband had fled upstairs on his own as we all arrived, but I felt sure he would have rather she'd been that way with him!

Something we WERE able to attend was thirty miles away in Southampton. This was the Lesbian and Gay Christian Movement. We went a few times and were made welcome, but it was a sixty mile journey there and back, and the meetings were of variable interest. It was also a bit of a ghetto, if you like. It seemed a shame for it to have to be a special "gay" meeting. Why couldn't everyone just be together?

All in all, we had to leave the Church behind once again, save for a friendship with an elderly couple, Mick and Peter, from the Poole Meeting of the Quakers.

Mick and Peter invited us to their house in Branksome several times when he would play the piano to entertain us before dinner. He could busk in the style of Russ Conway or Joe Henderson so that was very appealing to me. For my part, I would try to entertain them with my stories, and these were happy times.

Later that year, we really felt we wanted to make some kind of commitment, no formal method being available, so we invited Mick and Peter, along with Peter Martin from Southampton to a little ceremony in our front room. Peter Martin gave a blessing.

Michael started to help a lot with Tables Disco. It was a mail order business involving packing the tapes in jiffy bags to be posted out. Michael did a lot of this and then, when Peter and I came up with another idea for a new tape, Michael featured in photos and articles in more or less every national and regional newspaper in Britain. The new tape was called "Fear of Flying" and took us in another direction. We engaged a local hypnotherapist to record a tranquil, soothing message to calm the nerves of anyone facing a flight with fear.

A London PR firm came on board, and an excellent press release went out all over the place, resulting in widespread coverage. I'd photographed Michael holding up the tape next to a plane at Bournemouth Airport, and that's why his photo was everywhere!

Business was booming (for the moment) and my departure from teaching looked to be near.

Michael and I took a flight of our own. We went to Florida, to Walt Disney World where the EPCOT Center had just opened. This was an attraction called "World Showcase", set around a huge lake. Walt Disney World itself occupied a site of 42 square miles altogether, including the Magic Kingdom, Sleeping Beauty's Castle, Tomorrowland and the rest. Everywhere you went, you met Mickey Mouse. The funny thing was, however, that you could never see two of him at once. You'd keep seeing him every time you arrived in a new Land, or just turned a corner. There must have been thirty or more actors dressed as Mickey, but it was so cleverly organised that he just seemed to have beaten you to it when you went somewhere new.

We saw wonderful Parades and spectacular shows, rode on exhilarating rides, and ate American ice cream sundaes. However, one of my sayings is "enough is as good as a feast". I think it's safe to say that after a few days, it was all becoming a bit relentless. We were well and truly Mickeyed-out.

In the middle of the lake was an island filled with wonderful wildlife. The birds and animals there were not electric, but real. Best of all, Mickey and Minnie didn't seem to have discovered it. I have some beautiful pictures I took there of the most gorgeous flamingos with brilliant pink feathers.

<u>1988</u>

Nurses were awarded a 15% pay rise, and house prices in Norwich increased by 50% in just one year. A new law allowed pubs to open all day, and Ian Paisley denounced Pope John Paul II as the Antichrist. Edwina Currie declared that most of Britain's eggs were infected with salmonella, and would subsequently resign as health minister. Inflation was now down to 4.9%.

Hello Magazine was launched in a foretaste of today's celebrity culture, whereby people seem to be famous not for their talent, but just for being famous. Television host Russell Harty died, along with Whack-O comedian and actor Jimmy Edwards. Gardener Percy Thrower and Carry On actor Charles Hawtrey also passed away. I had once seen Charles Hawtrey in panto at Swindon, and I don't know when I have ever seen anyone "walk through" his role with such complete disinterest and disdain.

This was the year of another huge change, as I finally left teaching for good. We felt the educational tape business was strong enough for me to do so. Little did we know!

My brother Peter was always very black and white about everything. He didn't really appreciate nuance. Anyway, he was convinced that teaching was changing so much and this, coupled with the introduction of computers which neither of us could understand, brought about the decision. It was quite a moment when I took my class into the assembly hall for the very last time. I can honestly say I was overwhelmed with the number of presents and cards from parents and children. I still have all the cards, and the little sign which was displayed at the front of my desk inscribed "Mr C Webb". It was an even more pivotal moment when my very last salary cheque arrived. Now my only income would be what my brother and I could create through our own endeavours with our Tables Disco tapes and cds.

Before I move on to other more interesting things, I must go back one day to the day BEFORE my last as a teacher. My penultimate day at Winton Junior was memorable, to say the least.

I was always keen on outings. I guess I saw them as a way of making the children's learning entertaining. Having given in my notice, there was really no need for me to organise anything else. I was now leaving the profession, and could just coast along to the end without a great deal of effort.

Could I? I didn't think like that. If only I had.

I arranged a day trip for my class to Durlston, just beyond Swanage. My colleague and good friend Joan Callen accompanied me, and we hired a double decker bus from Bournemouth Corporation. When we arrived, we walked down to the Great Globe, past the Castle and along to the lighthouse. Up the hill and along the coast path we went, until we stopped for our packed lunch.

We sang songs on the hillside, and I'd prepared some games and a quiz. Finally, we walked back to the bus for what would be my very last journey with a group of children.

Carefully counting them all on board, we set off down the road from the Castle towards Swanage and home. We'd only travelled a hundred yards when CRACK! A huge tree branch SMASHED into the top deck of the bus with a tremendous explosive sound. Suddenly the whole of the top deck was filled with little pieces of shattered glass flying around among the screaming children.

The bus stopped, we all got out and congregated on the side of the road. Children were screaming, Joan and I were shaking, the driver was as shattered as the glass of his bus.

Did I say we sang songs during the lunch break on the hillside near the lighthouse?

Now Joan and I sang more songs with the children for nearly TWO HOURS while another bus was brought from Bournemouth. We finally arrived back at school in the early evening to a group of very distressed parents.

The next day, I left teaching.

What a way to end a career!

<u>1989</u>

A "fatwa" (order to kill) was issued against Salman Rushdie for writing his book "The Satanic Verses", and he had to go into hiding. 94 people were killed in the Hillsborough disaster at a football stadium in Sheffield, and the business of the House of Commons was televised for the first time. 27 million watched favourite character Alan Bradley being killed by a Blackpool tram in Coronation Street, a record audience for a "soap".

The SDP and the Liberals officially merged, being renamed Liberal Democrats, and Archbishop of Canterbury Robert Runcie suggested the Pope could become spiritual leader of a united church.

<u>1990</u>

The German supermarket chain Aldi opened its first UK store in Birmingham, France banned the import of British beef, and there were numerous more IRA bombings. Margaret Thatcher resigned as Conservative leader and Prime Minister and was replaced by John Major. The last coalmine in the Rhondda valley finally closed, and Princess

Eugenie was born. Toothy actor Terry Thomas died, and author Roald Dahl also passed away.

I went to America again, this time on my own. Mike and Judy were still living at Chappaqua upstate from New York and I spent a few days with them. I also spent some time in Boston, which I liked a lot. I saw the bridge in Boston Park where the memorable scene in "The Parent Trap" was filmed with Maureen O'Hara and Hayley Mills and I saw Debbie Reynolds in "The Unsinkable Molly Brown" at the theatre there. I travelled quite a bit around the area on the metro, going out to Harvard with its many bookshops and the University.

This was the year of my 40th birthday. We were still working hard on our educational tapes business, and had now made everything into cds which were the latest thing. Sales were becoming more difficult to achieve, and the advertising was getting too expensive. On one fateful occasion, we bought a full page ad in a Sunday supplement, which we often did by then, at a cost of £12000. This was an enormous risk, but it had become the only way we could get sales. Usually the cost would be covered by the income plus a bit more, which made the profit for us to live on. If you spend £12K on the ad and it brings an income of £13K, everything is fine. But what do you do if the ad makes a loss? How do you pay the bill, and how do you carry on running the business if that's the only way of getting sales?

This particular time, the sales were pretty much non-existent – and we had a bill of £12K to pay.

Our parents baled us out to the tune of the full £12K that was owing, saying that they would just leave us that much less in our inheritances. They also pointed out that they could only do it the once!

This raises the question as to where would we be today if they hadn't done that, and it shows why I continue to be careful with money. When you've been on the edge, so to speak, you don't want to go anywhere near it again.

It also raises the question of what would we have done if our parents didn't have £12 000, which many parents would not.

One of the lessons I learned from my mother which I am very grateful for was the story of Mr Micawber. She often reminded me of Charles Dickens' account of his fictional character's way of life.

"Income one pound. Expenditure nineteen shillings and sixpence. Result, happiness. Income one pound. Expenditure twenty shillings and sixpence. Result misery."

Would it not be better for young folk to be taught that nowadays?

Regarding the educational tapes and cds, the question arose as to how we could continue without so much risk. As it happened, I'd seen a fundraising scheme someone was running, and thought we could adapt it for our Tables Disco cds. Eventually, we moved to this new model whereby we sent a mailing letter to 27000 primary schools inviting them to bulk buy our cds and then sell them to the parents at a profit, thereby raising money for their school fund.

It cost around £1000 each time to join in with a bulk mailing to schools, but schools were ordering 50 or 100 copies of the cd as a result, often spending several hundred pounds with us. Now the risk was lower, and the profit was higher. We were on our way again.

We had a small 40th birthday party for me at home in Colehill and my brother Peter came, along with my college friend Alun and our Quaker friends Mick and Peter.

1991

The Provisional Irish Republican Army launched a mortar attack on 10 Downing Street, blowing in all the windows of the Cabinet Room. Victoria and Paddington Stations were also bombed. The World Wide Web was invented and the first website went live. "The Big Issue" was launched, due to the rapid increase in the numbers of homeless and rough sleepers. John Major outlined his vision for a "classless society".

Two IRA terrorists shot their way out of Brixton Prison, and two more accidentally killed themselves while trying to bomb St Albans. Thousands of shops defied trading laws by opening on a Sunday, and the first PC World store opened in Croydon. Freddie Mercury died of AIDS.

My brother Peter discovered a recording of a survivor of the Titanic. We made it into a sort of documentary and sold the recordings to schools, museums, libraries and individuals. One of my regrets is that I didn't apply myself enough to the Titanic idea. Looking back, I'm sure we could have made more of it, but I think I was satisfied with the rolling income from the schools' fundraising scheme and didn't see the need to branch out.

<u>1992</u>

The Queen, in her Ruby Jubilee Year, experienced her "annus horribilis" after several royal divorces and the fire at Windsor Castle. John Major won a fourth successive term for the Conservatives, and Neil Kinnock resigned as Labour Leader to be replaced by John Smith. Margaret Thatcher entered the House of Lords. Most retailers ceased selling vinyl lps, and comedians Frankie Howerd and Benny Hill passed away.

Who can forget Frankie Howerd saying "The number one thing you need in showbusiness is sincerity. If you can fake that, you've got it made!"

Britain's first ecumenical church, Christ the Cornerstone, was opened at Milton Keynes. It is still running today, with the C of E, Baptists, Methodists, Roman Catholics and United Reformed Churches all working together in harmony.

<u>1993</u>

Meridian Television started broadcasting on ITV and The Observer was bought by Guardian Media Group. The QVC shopping channel was launched. IRA bombings continued and The Queen announced that Buckingham Palace would open to the public. "Breakfast at Tiffanys" actress Audrey Hepburn died in Switzerland, along with comedian Les Dawson nearer to home.

Do we need reminding of Les Dawson's famous line?

"I took the wife to the Chamber of Horrors at Madame Tussauds. The attendant said to me 'Keep the Missus moving will you sir, only we're trying to stocktake.'"

I think I mentioned earlier on that my piano playing in assemblies was better than Les Dawson's – but only just.

"Breakfast at Tiffanys" was, and still remains, Michael's favourite film. With Andy Williams' "Moon River" recording of the film's haunting them song being one of my favourite tracks, there is another connection between us.

Stage Five: Touring Puppeteer.

In which I experience major grief for the first time, Michael joins me on the road as travelling puppeteers, and we create "Fantasy Florists". Read on to discover why!

<u>1994</u>

The Channel Tunnel opened. However, all our railways ground to a halt during a massive strike by 4000 signal staff. Tony Blair became Labour Leader and the Sunday Trading Act was passed. Another German supermarket chain, Lidl, opened their first ten stores in the UK, and Edwina Currie published her novel "A Parliamentary Affair".

The age of consent for male homosexuals was lowered from 21 to 18, and was set at 16 for females, thereby recognising the existence of lesbianism for the first time. Either Queen Victoria or the horses, or both, would have been terribly frightened!

Diver Tom Daley was born and Born Free actor Bill Travers died, along with famous cook Fanny Cradock, and entertainer Roy Castle. We would go on to get to know Roy's wife Fiona a decade later, meeting her frequently at showbiz events.

My mother died. This was the first time I'd had to deal with major grief, with the death of someone so close. Peter was a great strength and we dealt with everything as two brothers, supporting our father through it all. The greatest strength to me, however, was Michael. I remember several outings into the Dorset countryside where we would sit together and I would talk and he would listen. The most memorable was the time when we sat overlooking Durdle Door for quite a long while. My mother had suffered a series of strokes and had ended her days in a dreadful "home" at Bassett on the northern edge of Southampton. I think the time at Durdle Door might have been a turning point, as from that moment things started to change as regards the puppet shows. Within six months of my mother's death, I had contacted the agent of BBC Radio comedian and impersonator Peter Goodwright.

To cut a long story short, he came down to a recording studio (the same one we used for Tables Disco) and recorded lots of different voices for two different puppet productions that Michael and I would go on to create – The Fruitcake Mystery and The Puppet Factory.

Peter Goodwright was a lovely man. His house was called Dru-Wry, the kind of name that's just crying out for you to ask "Why is it called that?" which I naturally did. "It's named after a famous saying", he told me. "The remark that I've heard more times than any other in my life in showbusiness – Don't Ring Us – We'll Ring You!"

Soon, Michael came up with the idea that he should leave his catering job at Flight Refuelling and join me on the road. He's always the one that comes up with the most major changes for us. Anyway, for the next three years we toured the country's primary schools together, very quickly gaining an impression of the way things were in general in the education system.

Everywhere we went, we came across the number one fetish of UK primary school teachers – bottoms! Almost all teachers were female. Most schools we visited had no male teachers at all, or occasionally just one.

We would set everything up in the school hall and then the teachers would bring all the children in. The headmistress would be calling out "on your bottoms" many times as they arrived, meaning that they were to sit on the floor, not kneeling up at all. This happened more or less everywhere we went.

In some schools a woman would just call out "bottoms" repeatedly. On one occasion, the headmistress said "Children! I don't think James has got a bottom, because, if he had, he would be sitting on it!"

At another school, our van was too big to go into the small space in the staff car park. The secretary took a look and announced "You'll need to park with your bottom sticking out."

<u>1995</u>

The Queen and the Duke of Edinburgh visited Northern Ireland for the first time since the IRA's ceasefire, and the BBC began digital radio broadcasts. In local elections the Conservatives lost control of almost all councils, leaving them with just eight. Labour now controlled 155 and the Liberal Democrats 45. The Conservatives had no councils at all in Wales or Scotland.

The Pensions Act set out to equalise the retirement age for men and women over the next ten years. Cliff Richard received a knighthood, becoming Sir Cliff, and Larry Grayson, Kenny Everett and "Yes Minister" actor Paul Eddington all died. Paul Eddington had also starred in "The Good Life" with Penelope Keith, Felicity Kendall and Richard Briars in the days when we had quality comedy on the BBC. I had seen him on stage in the West End in 1984 in the original run of Michael Frayn's "Noises Off" during my year at London University.

We went to a major charity event at Bristol Hippodrome Theatre, Russ Conway's 70th Birthday. Many stars took part, and the host was none other than Peter Goodwright, who had recorded the voice-overs for our puppet shows two years earlier. The huge theatre was packed, and it was amazing to admire Peter Goodwright's comedy technique. He could deliver a line, walk to the side of the stage and lean against the proscenium arch while the audience laughed, and then stroll back to the middle again to deliver the next. He was in complete command of the event, and I was in awe of his ability. Stars taking part included Bob Monkhouse, Anita Harris, and Bernie Clifton.

Remember the clever line Bob Monkhouse wrote for Jack Benny? Here are some he would often use himself.

"When I was a boy, we used to knock on people's doors and run away. Nowadays we call that ParcelForce."

"You know you're getting older when the only thing you feel like exercising is caution."

Or his opening line ...

"As Henry the Eighth would say to each of his wives, I shall not keep you long."

Peter and I continued with our educational cd business, but once again it was starting to struggle a bit. How wonderful it would be to have a regular salary or wage that you could rely upon, coming in every month. Even more amazing would be to have paid holidays, sick pay, etc. but this was not to be. It had been our own choice to give all that up a few years before. One of Grandad Bath's favourite sayings was "He's made his bed and he'll have to lie on it".

To supplement the Tables Disco fundraising income, we carried on with our puppet shows in the schools, but the pay was relatively low and we were away on tour a lot.

Michael and I also went to Wootton Under Edge in Gloucestershire for Roger Welshman's wedding. He married Yasmin in a simple ceremony in the village church, and they were taken in a carriage to the village hall where there was a reception. Roger had asked me to give a speech. I tried to entertain, and can remember getting quite a few laughs!

<u>1996</u>

Arthur Scargill left the Labour Party to set up his own separate Socialist Labour Party, and British Rail was privatised. South West Trains was one of the first franchises to run under the strange new system which separated the running of the trains from the ownership and maintenance of the tracks. Now superseded by South Western Railway and amazingly as I write, the whole franchising system has been abandoned and the railways re-nationalised – by a Conservative government! This is due to the coronavirus pandemic.

The IRA ended their much vaunted "ceasefire" by bombing Canary Wharf and a London bus. The Local Government Act created new separate Unitary Authorities for Wales and Scotland, and in the local elections the Conservatives lost another 578, taking Labour to a new high of eleven thousand seats across the UK. In government nationally, the Conservative majority was now one!

Charles and Diana divorced, as did Andrew and Sarah, and Dolly the Sheep was cloned.

By the end of the year 4% of the population had internet access.

Hollywood actress Greer Garson died. She had starred in my favourite film "The Happiest Millionaire" alongside Fred MacMurray, Gladys Cooper and Tommy Steele. Other notable deaths included Christopher Robin (Milne), Beryl Reid, and jazz club owner Ronnie Scott.

Leslie Crowther also passed away shortly after a serious accident on the M5. Always regarded as rather a second-rate comedian, he did in fact have many talents. I had been there when he gave a wonderful evening of entertainment in aid of the Theatre Royal Bath. In a varied and wide-ranging one man show, he single-handedly held the audience for two hours, performing everything from comic songs, to Betjeman poems and passage from Shakespeare.

If nothing else, I'm sure you remember Leslie Crowther's television adverts "I can't tell Stork from butter!"

Do they still have Stork margarine nowadays?

Another family death was that of cousin Ena. She was John's mother, Jonathan and Samantha's grandmother, and Cyril's wife. Even though she was becoming elderly herself, she ran her Golden Years Club for the old folks of Wimborne, meeting at the Liberal Hall. Towards the end, she herself was older than most of the members!

As we carried on with our tours to schools with our puppets, we didn't yet know that it would also be the start of our life in professional showbusiness, something that would become our "baby" and would grow under our nurturing. Something that is now sadly missing from our lives as we have closed down all our business projects, I have retired, and Michael is volunteering at the Wimborne Food Bank and the Trussell Trust charity shop.

Back then, however, Michael joining me in the school shows was an enormous change but it worked out very well. Using some of the voice tracks Peter Goodwright had recorded, we created a show called The Fruitcake Mystery, which featured the two of us with four different kinds of puppets – rod puppets, glove puppets, vent puppets, and string puppets (marionettes). We performed for an hour in big school halls to up to 400 children at a time, and then gave a demonstration and question time on how the puppets worked, etc. The bookings took us all over England. We didn't offer it to schools in Wales or Scotland, but the English travel was enough. We seemed to be popular in Newcastle, which was not overly convenient for us living on the south coast!

We would stay each night at Travelodges and dine at Little Chef. Life was hard. The journeys were relentless, the meals repetitive, and the fees we could charge were low, especially when split between two. We played around 150 schools in the first year, and soon discovered a major problem. Those who liked what we did would say "What are you doing NEXT year?" In other words, we would need to come up with something new and completely different – and prepare all this at the same time as fulfilling THIS year's bookings!

We came up with another show called The Puppet Factory, using more of the voices Peter Goodwright had recorded. At the time, everything seemed to be a "factory" as far as advertising was concerned, and we thought this would be a good title.

The show consisted of a story taking place in a puppet factory, and gave the opportunity once again to feature our four different kinds of puppets, along with a demonstration, etc. We engaged Keith Daly, the chap who had worked a lot with Peter and me on Tables Disco, to write and record some new songs, and we acquired a whole new cast of puppets from a showbusiness colleague Mel Harvey, who was currently touring small theatres with his children's show Presto the Magic Rabbit.

We played another 150 or so schools the following year with our new show, but then, as you can guess, the same problem arose. What could we do the NEXT year? In other words, it looked like we were expected to create ANOTHER new show – or else come up with a different way of making a living.

Another problem was the major setback we received when our van was broken into in the Travelodge car park at Ilford. We both thought we'd heard something outside the window during the night, and when we got up, we found the van back doors had been forced open and our amplifier and speakers stolen. This meant not only the loss of the equipment, but an expensive repair to the van, and more to the point, the loss of the income from the next few shows.

The response of the schools varied. Most were very sympathetic and asked us to rearrange a date as soon as we were able. One headmistress merely stated that, as we had let her down, she wouldn't ever be booking us again.

This whole episode led us to create Fantasy Florists. We disguised the van with florists' signs, which we hoped would give the impression that the only thing inside would be some flowers, vases and leaves! It certainly worked, as we were not broken into again. (Our large van for our big children's/pantomime shows WAS broken into a few years later, and was also set on fire. Such is life in Britain.)

Schools were often surprised to see a florists' van coming up their drive when they hadn't ordered any flowers. It looked completely realistic, with a fictional phone number, a catchy slogan, and pictures of flowers adorning the side panels and both the back doors!

By now, we'd travelled over fifty thousand miles in our small van and it was getting a bit tired. There wasn't anything to spare with which to buy a new one, so something had to give.

As an Equity member, I managed to get quite a bit of voice over work. I could speak clearly and with expression, and could put over a story, or so people said. This certainly provided an extra income, and didn't involve much travelling other than to London. Not being much of a Union man myself, I have to put on record that Equity supported me and managed to recover a fee I was owed that someone hadn't paid. I think £1500, as I recall. So well done them!

They took the guy to court and won. It was a clear-cut case, as he had signed a contract for him to pay that fee.

As I said, we were beginning to wonder if there was a different way for us to earn a living. We wanted to be in showbusiness, and it's well known for being hand to mouth. Anyway, I can't really remember how, but we came in contact with a tour booker called Susannah Kraft, and she offered to book us into small theatres and arts centres. She came to one of our school shows to watch us from the back of the hall, as a kind of audition. She liked what she saw and was happy to take us on. Under her management, we played 35 theatres in 1996 including Wimborne Tivoli Theatre which had now reopened, plus theatres as far flung as Colwyn Bay, Bognor Regis, Watford, and Milton Keynes. This still involved much travel, but the income from each show was equivalent to three or four schools, and it was much more satisfying playing to the general public who had paid to come and see us. We were on the very edge of entering professional theatre touring. Little did we know what we would soon be doing.

On a personal note, and a very sad one, Michael was becoming increasingly distressed about the way his parents viewed him, so much so that he decided to write to them sending his undying love but saying that it would be better for us not to meet any more as it was proving too painful. His mother wrote back expressing similar love, but just saying they would respect our decision.

Michael is one of three. Stephen is the eldest, Shelagh is the youngest, and Michael is in the middle. As far as all of them were concerned, the problem was their father. I have already intimated how he used to bark instructions at his wife, Gina. All three children had found their upbringing most unpleasant to say the least. Stephen had severed all contact with the rest of the family, and Shelagh was struggling with issues of her own.

As a result of the exchange of letters between them, there was no more contact between Michael and his parents until we heard that Michael's mother was terminally ill with cancer. Tragically, we didn't see her or his father again, and did not attend either of their funerals. A big subject which cannot be aired here or given full justice. Suffice to say that the whole thing was enormously traumatic for all concerned.

Michael changed his name by Deed Poll, and from that date has been Michael Jones.

<u>1997</u>

Tony Blair won a landslide victory for New Labour with 418 seats. Where was Arthur Scargill's "Socialist Labour"? 160 vehicles were involved in a huge crash on the motorway near Bromsgrove, the Royal Yacht Britannia was decommissioned, and Diana died following a car crash in Paris.

There was a national outpouring of grief. She had been thought of as the "people's" princess. Michael and I were in

Okehampton at the time, a place we like in mid Devon. When we walked into the town square on the Sunday morning to buy the Sunday papers, we were astonished to see a great pile of wreaths laid on and around the war memorial. We couldn't imagine why, so asked when we went into the newsagents. "Diana has died" was the answer.

This was the year when J K Rowling published her first Harry Potter book - something I have never read. You may not be surprised to learn that I have never seen any of the films either. Always a rebel, I'm afraid!

The Revd W Audrey, writer of the Thomas the Tank Engine books died, together with poet Laurie Lee. Michael and I were later to make friends with the Producer of the "Thomas" television series, Simon Spencer, and keen readers will remember that I taught Laurie Lee's daughter at Painswick Primary School.

Cousin Muriel died in Wimborne. She had lost her husband Charles in 1981, as I have recorded, and since then her sister Kathleen had been living with her to keep her company. They were in Whitehouse Rd, the same road where my good friend David Green had lived with his parents. Michael and I see David and his partner William regularly for meals in each others' homes, and more recently for Sunday lunches at the Elstead Hotel in Bournemouth.

Stage Six:
Big Business in Showbusiness!

In which we make friends with Connie Creighton, and borrow £95 000 to take our first tentative steps into professional showbusiness as theatrical producers.

<u>1998</u>

Construction began of the infamous Millennium Dome, and the £2 coin was introduced. Herefordshire and Worcestershire were given back their original separate identities, having been the one county of "Hereford and Worcester" for the past 14 years.

In Ireland, the Good Friday Agreement was reached.

Nigella Lawson published her first cookery book, and vegetarian wife of Beatle Paul, Linda McCartney died. Other deaths here in the UK included writer Frank Muir and poet Ted Hughes, while Hollywood lost one of my favourite actors Roddy McDowall.

I was starting to feel that our future lay in professional showbusiness, not so much on the stage, but behind the scenes as impresarios (producers). I saw in The Stage Newspaper an event advertised at the Southport Theatre for professional networking among producers, agents, etc. and decided to travel north to attend, not knowing what to expect. I didn't know anyone who'd be there, but I thought some kind of benefit might come out of it. I remember spending £70 on a return train ticket, which was a lot for us to find, and thinking I must make sure I got more than £70 value out of going there.

As it turned out, there were three benefits, maybe more.

Firstly, I met a theatre manager and got chatting. I asked what shows he had coming up at his venue, and he said the next was an evening with pianist entertainer, Bobby Crush. He said he'd booked the show on a First Call, and I of course didn't know what that was. He explained all the various terms that theatres use to book shows and I've set them all down in Appendix 6.

The second benefit gained from going to the event at Southport was discovering Encore Magazine, billed as "for the showbusiness professional". This was not generally on sale and I wouldn't have known about it unless I'd gone there that day. It turned out to be a mine of information about what was going on in the theatre industry behind the scenes, and we became regular subscribers. We knew The Stage Newspaper, but that was mainly aimed at actors, singers, etc. Encore Magazine was for management.

The third great benefit was making friends with Connie Creighton. I met her having coffee in between the various presentations. She was personable and charming, and had travelled up there from Bournemouth as it happened. I recognised her as I'd seen her on television many times in

The Sooty Show which she'd presented for 23 years, firstly with Harry Corbett, and more latterly with his son Matthew. Connie did all the Sooty theatre tours as well.

We went on to become good friends, often visiting each other's homes, which were only five miles apart. Once our friendship was really established, and our touring theatre business was properly under way, Connie would have our schedule on the wall next to the phone in her hall, and would follow us round "in spirit", imagining us at Newcastle, Blackpool, Aberystwyth, Norwich, Plymouth – or wherever we were on that particular day.

Michael and I would often meet Connie at Beales for coffee (the top floor coffee shop and the whole store now gone). These were very pleasant occasions and the conversation really flowed, but it was constantly interrupted by people coming up to her merely just to say how lovely it was to see her, or to ask for her autograph. She was endlessly charming and patient but I think, really, she greatly enjoyed the attention.

As I said, we'd put together a second version of our puppet show and called it The Puppet Factory. This had been the basis of our second year touring the schools. Once again, the two of us appeared on stage in routines with big vent-style puppets, marionettes, rod and glove puppets. We got children up to take part, and featured newly written special songs and comedy routines.

After our first small-scale theatre tour booked by Susannah Kraft, The Puppet Factory gave us a second offering for another tour.

Susannah booked another sequence of venues for us and we played Bridport Arts Centre, Tamworth Arts Centre, where my cousin Rosemary came to watch, the Roses Theatre at Tewkesbury, and the Arc Theatre, Trowbridge. We actually opened the tour at the Trowbridge Arc Theatre and, in fact, opened that theatre as well, performing the very first professional show they'd had there.

Our new friend Connie Creighton came along to the Trowbridge show, where we actually had a full house. It wasn't very big, maybe about 160 seats, and I guess the full house was more to do with us being the first ever show at that new theatre rather than the attraction of seeing Michael and me on the stage. Whatever the reason, we were quite nervous about performing in front of Connie and her husband John. She'd been appearing at the country's biggest theatres for 23 years and done numerous television shows. John had been a puppeteer also, working Sweep alongside Sooty and his friends. In the event, the show went really well, and afterwards Connie said she'd loved every minute. What a lovely lady.

Here's the review from the Corby Evening Telegraph following our appearance at The Willows there.

"The show was full of technical wizardry and both youngsters and parents had a good time. Technical

Manager of the complex Richard Glen said, 'It was a great show. It was very clever. It was not just your average puppet show where you just see the puppets, it was very interactive.'"

On the 12 December, my 48th birthday, we appeared at the Compass Theatre, Ickenham where we performed The Puppet Factory twice, playing to two full houses. We weren't to know that the Compass Theatre would be our base in years to come for auditions and rehearsals for all our big nationwide children's theatre tours and pantomimes.

What a year this was. Enthused by our friendship with Connie, our own success in theatres with The Puppet Factory, and a need to expand further (in business terms, not waistline), somehow we started to present The Bachelors Show.

Observant readers will recall that, back in the sixties when I was a teenager and everyone else was either following The Beatles or The Stones, my favourites were The Bachelors. As I related earlier, Con, Dec and John had split in 1984, with Con and Dec performing alongside a new partner for a while and then just as a duo. John Stokes had disappeared from the scene.

Now we heard that he was back with two new compatriots, forming a polished, stylish trio that were getting terrific reviews. I set about finding them, or their representation. This was quite a task, and I can't now say how I did it. Persistence has always been one of my bywords. Anyway, I discovered they were appearing in their own new version of "The Bachelors Show" at Heywood Civic Theatre on the outskirts of Manchester. A one-nighter. Quite a contrast to their dates as the original trio when they would play the London Palladium and sixteen-week seasons at the biggest theatres in the land.

I travelled to Manchester and managed to go backstage to meet the new threesome in their dressing room. We must have clicked somehow as, after only a few weeks' negotiations, they agreed for Michael and me to produce them on tour. All we needed was a support act for the first half. I'd seen comedienne Dotty Wayne advertised in a showbusiness directory and thought comedy might be a good foil for the slick, polished harmony of our top-of-the-bill. I tracked her down to a summer season in Bridlington and again travelled there to meet her. Looking back I can see (a) how determined I was and (b) what an incredible amount of travel professional showbusiness involves.

All I can remember about my encounter with Dottie at Bridlington is that I developed toothache while there! I also remember a young man, an acrobat, backstage who was a great talent in the show and an absolute Adonis in the dressing room. I don't think he had the least idea the effect he was having on me!

I hit it off with Dottie and she put me in touch with her agent, Sylvia Thorley, who lived on the Isle of Wight. Tragically, Sylvia was terminally ill with leukaemia at the time, and was conducting her business from her hospital bed. A deal was done, and Dottie became a regular fixture in our variety shows over the following decade. We opened "The Bachelors Show with John Stokes" at the Alexandra Theatre, Bognor Regis, a venue that Michael and I had appeared at with our puppets and one that would become a regular haunt for us, and miraculously Sylvia was able to come to our opening night.

Dottie's act was just a little risqué. She would announce after a while that she was wearing new knickers especially for the occasion. "I call them my harvest festivals," she would say. "All is safely gathered in".

My two cousins Rosemary and Jennifer travelled all the way to Bognor to support us in our new venture - The Bachelors Show. Really, they were both into rock music of different kinds, and close harmony singing involving girls' names like Charmaine, Ramona, Diane etc. was not really their scene. It was really lovely of them to come and, in the event, they thoroughly enjoyed the whole show. Talent, polish and sheer professionalism will always win the day!

We took John Stokes and his version of The Bachelors to numerous theatres all over the UK for the next ten years, taking in iconic venues like Leeds City Varieties, home of the long-running tv show The Good Old Days, and finally ending up doing a short season with them at the North Pier Theatre, Blackpool in 2008. Coincidentally, that year the original three were once again riding high in the charts, reaching number 8 in the top ten with a "best of" cd album.

That certainly helped ticket sales for our shows in Blackpool.

<u>1999</u>

The Euro was launched, with Britain's Labour Government deciding to keep the pound. Unemployment was now the lowest for 20 years. A minimum wage was introduced for the first time, set at £3.60/hr. Prince Edward married Sophie Rhys-Jones, and Charles Kennedy became leader of the Liberal Democrats. Construction of the London Eye began on the South Bank, and the Midland Bank became HSBC.

In a change from the activities of the IRA, a bomb was detonated at the Admiral Duncan pub in Soho targeting the gay community, killing and seriously injuring the customers just for being "different".

Leader of the Roman Catholics in the UK, Cardinal Basil Hume died, and we also lost author and thinker Iris Murdoch.

Showbusiness lost Rod Hull and his Emu (which may not have been too much of an upset for Michael Parkinson!), Quentin Crisp, and Johnnie Morris. Do you remember Animal Magic? And do you also remember Johnnie as the Hot Chestnut Man?

Multi-talented singer, actor and composer Anthony Newley died. We had met him a few years before at the Café Royal when his manager Peter Charlesworth had invited us backstage after one of Anthony's cabaret performances. At the time, Michael and I were still just doing our puppet shows in the schools, albeit nationwide. This star of Broadway, West End, Hollywood, and Las Vegas spent the time with us asking all about OUR shows and showing real interest. How's that for modesty?

Newley's manager Peter Charlesworth also managed Joan Collins. A few years later, when we were well established impresarios, Peter Charlesworth invited me to his mews house in Holland Park to discuss the possibility of us producing Joan's "evening with" theatre tour. We'd already had dealings with him by then as he managed Melvyn Hayes who worked for us a few times, and Peter had been kind enough to say working with us was an "absolute pleasure". Dame Joan's tour wasn't to be under our mangement, for a number of reasons, and in the end we were told she'd more or less produced it herself, with her husband Percy selling the programmes in the foyer, as I would always do myself at every theatre we played.

My niece Rachel, elder daughter of Peter and Barbara, married Sean Carroll and we went to the wedding.

We went on holiday to Malta. We have rarely travelled abroad, but this was a bargain break advertised, and we thought we would try it. As it turned out, we were to return to Malta ten more times! We love the whole culture of the place, the warm climate during our winter, the welcoming people, and the laid-back lifestyle. Very Catholic, on more or less every corner of every street you will find a little shrine to the Blessed Virgin.

<u>2000</u>

Millennium celebrations were held all over the UK, mostly beginning just after midnight and going on into the early hours. We were at the Kings Head in Wimborne where we had a nice dinner and then went out into the Square at midnight. We'd met a very nice couple during the evening, a mother and daughter from Paris, and had chatted to them quite a bit, so they were the first people we socialised with in the new year. We were home by 12 30!

The Millennium Dome was opened by the Queen and later in the year, the Queen Mother celebrated her 100th birthday.

On May Day there were riots by anti-capitalists and Winston Churchill's statue was daubed with graffiti (not for the last time). Trams returned to Greater London for the first time since 1952, with the opening of Tramlink in Croydon.

The first "reality" Big Brother tv programme was shown. Where once we could have watched the greatest talents in the world of entertainment, now we could see "ordinary" people sitting around, doing nothing, swearing and occasionally arguing with each other. Come to think of it, we'd had "Till Death Us Do Part" in the 60s, which featured all I've just mentioned, but that was cleverly scripted and funny.

Sales of dvds passed one million.

The Church of England introduced Common Worship. One of the things I have always liked about Anglican Services is the beautiful poetry in the liturgy of the Book of Common Prayer. This had now been watered down and paraphrased to make it more "accessible". Numbers worshipping at the C of E continued to decline, however.

Dame Barbara Cartland died, and we also lost Sir John Gielgud and political broadcaster Robin Day.

My younger niece Nina married Mike in Southampton and we went to the wedding.

In Wimborne, cousin Cyril died. Cyril King was the husband of cousin Ena, who had passed away in 1996.

The puppet shows were becoming increasingly difficult. We were playing around 150 schools each year, as I said, plus a handful of theatres and arts centres. The latter were not a problem, but the schools were! We had to drive long distances in the van each day, visiting one school in the morning, packing everything back into the van over the lunchtime and then driving to another school for the afternoon. Unloading it all again, setting it all up in the afternoon school's hall, doing the second show, packing it all into the van again, and then driving another long distance to a Travelodge in which to stay, ready to do it all again the next day. We made about £100 profit on each show, so over the whole 150 schools in the year, we made about £1500 – or £7500 each. We'd have almost been better off on benefits.

As well as the journeys and days in the schools there were all the rehearsals beforehand, plus the endless admin work issuing the contracts, and the advertising and promotion to actually get the bookings.

The van had cost £7000, which had to be repaid out of the money coming in from the schools. We would soon need another one.

The show itself lasted an hour, but we were in each school three hours altogether - an hour setting up before, an hour doing the performance, and another hour dismantling afterwards. The journey to each school took another one to two hours also.

At a school over in Kent, near Maidstone, we'd had an exhausting time in the morning as everything had had to be carried up two flights of stairs. We hadn't had any time to eat our sandwiches in the van as we were due at the afternoon school at 1.00 pm to set everything up again there ready for a 2 pm performance.

Even though the school were expecting us, we arrived to find the gates locked and bolted. It took Michael quite a while to go in and get someone to come out with a key.

Once we did gain entry, by now 20 minutes late, we were shown the hall in which we were to perform. The entire floor was covered in slimy cabbage, bits of boiled potato and other discarded food. Several dinner ladies were dutifully sweeping it all up, the children who had scattered it all having left to go back to their classes.

Each school signed a contract stating that the hall would be available unobstructed for an hour before showtime.

There was no way that we could begin to put up our show until the floor was cleared, cleaned and dried. This took another 20 minutes. We hurried as fast as we could to put up the set, position all the puppets, put on our costumes and do our sound check with our microphones, and test the recorded sound system. We managed to get everything ready for the children and their teachers to come in, only about half an hour after the agreed show time, with several staff complaining about being made to wait.

To put things in perspective, we did also visit some wonderful schools where we were made very welcome and the staff were very complimentary about our performance.

Just as an example, and being naturally given to modesty, I will just quote Ewell Castle Junior School, Surrey:- "Brilliant! A real inspiration", and St Andrews Junior School, Lincoln:- "You kept the children enthralled for a full hour".

Lady St Mary School, Wareham sent a letter saying "You've been an inspiration", going on to describe all the puppets the children had made after our visit, and sending us photos and pictures the children had drawn themselves. Many schools used to do this.

Others, like Larks Hill School in West Yorkshire, also wrote to say that we'd sparked off wonderful creative writing.

Whenever we were in Yorkshire, we were able to visit my good friend Edith Calvert who by then was living in Skipton. I'd made friends with her when she came to Winton Junior as a special needs peripatetic teacher. She'd previously lived in Crete and had enjoyed some Greek meals in Bournemouth with Alun and me when Alun was visiting.

Over all though, as you can see, we would have gone to an early grave if we'd carried on like we were doing for very much longer.

We would have to find another way to earn a living. Susannah Kraft had booked us another tour of small theatres and arts centres with our Puppet Factory show. We did well with this and were well received by audiences. Like before in The Fruitcake Mystery, the two of us would appear on stage interacting with the audience and the puppets, inviting children up to take part in routines and songs, etc. We appeared at 23 theatres in all that year, including Watford Palace Theatre, Redditch Palace Theatre, and the Wolsey Theatre, Cheshunt. Those are just three that come to mind. Although the tour was profitable, it was extremely tiring with all the long distance driving involved, and it didn't make anywhere near enough for the two of us to live on.

What to do?

In the May of 2000, an ad appeared in The Stage newspaper giving details of a children's theatre company for sale. There was just a box number, and we decided to apply for details. We discovered it was playing theatres all over the country with traditional, panto-style shows like Pinocchio, Humpty Dumpty, and The Ugly Duckling. Each show had a cast of 5 actors, plus a Company Manager, and toured in a big van containing all the scenery and props. They performed matinees at big venues like The Kings Theatre Southsea, Leeds City Varieties Theatre, and Bolton Albert Halls.

The asking price for the company was £95000, to include all the scenery, props and costumes for three complete productions, the scripts, the music, the "goodwill" of 63 theatres booked going forward, plus two big long-wheelbase vans.

We had just £1000 in savings between us, but nevertheless decided to pursue the opportunity.

I was invited to go over to Pontypridd to the theatre there to see a matinee of Humpty Dumpty in Nursery Rhyme Land. When I arrived, the morning show was just finishing and the audience were streaming out into the street, several hundred of them. Young families were all leaving with smiles on their faces and a souvenir programme in their hands.

Just nearby, another crowd were gathered. These were waiting to go in to second house. I followed them in and sat at the back, clutching my complimentary ticket in my hand along with my own souvenir programme.

The show started. The scenery was bright, the costumes were colourful, the songs and dances were lively, and the young cast of five actors performed with gusto. After the show, I met the producer Steve, who was offering the company for sale.

He explained that he and his business partner Patrick were touring two productions at once. While this troupe were on the road with Humpty Dumpty, another similar crew were touring in another van with Hans Christian Andersen's The Ugly Duckling – the Musical. I could have gone to Bury St Edmunds to see them that same afternoon at the Theatre Royal there.

Steve and I had quite a thorough discussion re all the ins and outs of the business. While we were talking, the audience were all queuing up to have their photo taken with Humpty Dumpty for £3, or joining another queue to buy flashing wands, also £3 each. The theatre was humming with activity, and lots of money was changing hands.

I drove home to Dorset to talk everything over with Michael.

There was clearly a very viable business here, but incredible risk and responsibility. If you could manage to put all the shows together, engage and rehearse the cast, book the theatres, maintain and tour the vans, you could clearly make a good living.

But what if something went wrong? There were an infinite number of ways that could happen. A chain is only as strong as its weakest link, and one tiny element going awry could mean the whole tour going up in smoke.

We talked and talked. The overriding thing was that we were running out of energy doing the puppet shows in the schools, and we were barely scraping a living. We'd HAVE to come up with something else and this was clearly an opportunity.

I went to meet Steve again. I'd met him at the theatre in Pontypridd, but had not yet met Patrick, his business partner. They invited me to join them at the Tower Hotel in London, just below the famous Tower Bridge. We sat in the lounge for a couple of hours and talked and talked. They told me they had twelve people interested in acquiring their business, so there was no chance of negotiating the price down.

What they wanted most of all was someone whom they could trust to carry on the good name they'd established. They wanted someone who'd be capable of keeping everything going and fulfilling all the contracts they'd already signed with theatres for the next year or so. Somehow, I must have given them the impression that Michael and I were the ones who could do that.

Part of what convinced them was the fact that we were already producing The Bachelors Show at UK theatres and, in the same way that they'd invited me to their Humpty Dumpty Show at Pontypridd, we invited Steve to our Bachelors Show at The West Cliff Clacton. This went down a storm, and we ended with audience cheers and "More! More!" from the full house. Steve just said "Nice one, Derek" afterwards, playing his cards close to his chest!

However, shortly after the Clacton encounter, Steve and Patrick made it clear they would like US to take over their big production company. It was their baby, they were very proud of it, and they wanted it to continue in safe hands. So far, so good.

The only problem was, we didn't have ninety five thousand pounds! We had ONE thousand between us, as I've said.

We were delighted and amazed when they agreed to lend us the money in order for us to buy everything from them. In other words, we paid them £1000, signed the contract, and OWED them £94 000. Everything was ours!

We agreed we would gradually pay it all over to them out of the income from the shows, until it was all paid off. There would be virtually nothing for ourselves until this was achieved.

The first show that we did was at the Beaufort Theatre, Ebbw Vale. The Pinocchio tour was already on the road on the day we took over, so we drove over there to meet the cast and watch the show that was already up and running. There was a good house, the programme and souvenir sales were very strong, and the whole thing was a success.

The next day we repeated everything at the theatre at Aberdare, the company went on to the next theatre, and we drove home. We were on our way!

Little did we know what was in store. It is fair to say that if we HAD known, we would not have bought the business. However, it's a jolly good job we did, all in all, as I can't imagine what we would have done if we hadn't.

<u>2001</u>

There were more violent anti-capitalist protests in London, and Deputy Prime Minister John Prescott (in 2020 now Lord Prescott of Kingston upon Hull) hit out in retaliation when a protester threw an egg at him. There were race riots in Burnley and Bradford.

The age of consent was lowered to 16 for gay men, bringing in equality with heterosexuals, and gay women.

2001 was, of course, the year of the terrible 9/11 terrorist attack by Al Qaeda on the World Trade Centre in New York. Michael and I had been to the top of this building when we were there in 1995.

Nearer to home, there was a foot and mouth disease crisis, Beatle George Harrison died, and Sir Harry Secombe passed away. We'd seen Harry Secombe in a revival of "Pickwick" at Chichester Festival Theatre a few years before, and keen readers will remember my friend Stephen's first selection from the World Record Club in 1969.

2001 was the year my two great nephews were born. Joe was born in July to Rachel and Sean. Jack was born in October to Nina and Mike. I was now a Great Uncle. (Upon entering a Civil Partnership with Michael in 2007, they would then become great nephews to Michael as well, with him being their Great Uncle also.)

Unknown to us at the time, we now had a nephew, Michael's sister Shelagh's son, Max. Shelagh had married Gary the previous year, and their son Max was born in 2001.

As the year began, we realised we would need help re all the admin that was needed back at base to keep the shows on the road. There were endless contracts to prepare and sign, there was VAT to account for, and phone calls coming in every hour. We advertised for an administrator and found Shirley.

Shirley Robson agreeing to work for us was one of those "meant to be" moments. No one could have done it all better. She quickly gained a genuine interest in all we were doing and applied herself diligently to everything that came her way. The only thing admin-wise that I kept for myself was the accounting. Firstly, I enjoyed it, and secondly, it's the only way to keep a grip on how things are financially. If you do the accounts yourself, you have a clear picture of the constantly changing situation, and running any kind if business is all about cash flow. i.e. you have to have enough cash in hand to meet bills as they arise. I had a big ledger analysis book with thirteen columns on the outgoings side and five on the income side. I filled in everything by hand, taking the VAT out of the figures where it had been applied and accounting for that separately on the edge of each page ready for Shirley to fill in the quarterly VAT returns when required.

In March of 2001 we held a party to mark my 50th birthday which had taken place in December 2000. We hired the main room at the Allendale Centre in Wimborne and 50 guests attended. Connie Creighton entertained on stage with Sooty, David Conway from The Three Monarchs played the harmonica, and a young double act Ian Adams and Vivienne McMaster sang music hall songs. My brother Peter came, along with college friends, local neighbours, friends from my teaching days, even including Edith who travelled all the way from Skipton. Wonderful.

Our new Administrator Shirley came with her husband Sandy, and I think they were enjoying their introduction to showbusiness!

Steve and Patrick were keeping an eye on us as we got going. There was an awful lot to learn and part of our contract with them was that they would act as consultants until our huge debt was paid off.

We continued with Pinocchio with a mostly new cast. We held auditions in west London at a room we hired in a theatre there, the Compass Theatre, the same one where Michael and I had appeared a couple of years previously and played to a full house.

One actor carried on with us from before, providing continuity, and the others were new, our own choice. We also had to engage a choreographer and director, plus a company manager to drive the van and oversee the production in each venue. We did the very same thing with The Ugly Duckling. It was like a plate spinning act – keeping both plates spinning in the air at the same time.

Disaster struck on the third day of the Ugly Duckling tour. Vandals (arsonists) set our van on fire, containing all the scenery, props and costumes. It was parked overnight at Bishops Stortford in Essex, ready to do shows at Harlow Playhouse. We had to rush over there, hire a van to replace our own which was now burnt, and transfer everything into the new van. All the equipment had been fireproofed (!) and there was minor smoke damage, nothing more.

There was extra work re insurance etc. but miraculously the tour was not interrupted, and the show went on at Harlow. Although we'd got through that time, it only demonstrated what a knife edge everything was on.

I'll write a little about The Ugly Duckling show, which I'll use as an example of what our children's shows and pantomimes were like. When we bought the company, we adapted the script a little to bring out Hans Christian Andersen's original message, namely the problems of being seen as "different". It was a complete musical and we moved some of the songs and scenes around to provide a bit more pacing. The cast of five worked hard, really reaching the audience in the participation numbers, performing the dances with style, and holding the audience's attention throughout. We added a "proper" finale walk-down and each time got a similar reaction to what our talented cast were getting in our Bachelors variety show! "Now that's what I call a show!"

Here, as an example, is an idea of what we did with The Ugly Duckling show over the years ...

In the first year, 2001, we presented it at 8 theatres including Sunderland Empire, Salisbury City Hall, Weymouth Pavilion and Jersey Opera House.

In 2002, we toured it to 88 theatres with another new cast. We took it from Yeovil Octagon to Perth City Hall, from Worthing Pavilion to Theatr Cymru Llandudno, from Weston Super Mare Playhouse to Belfast Mossley Pavilion, and from The Marina Theatre Lowestoft to the Lyceum Theatre Crewe, plus 80 others.

The following year, 2003, we played it at 9 more theatres including the Embassy Theatre Skegness and 4 days at Jersey Opera House.

In 2006, our Ugly Duckling Show played 16 more theatres including Fleetwood Marine Hall, Buxton Opera House, and Bournemouth Pavilion.

In 2008 we took it out again to 24 theatres including Peterborough Broadway, Lichfield Garrick, Doncaster Civic, and The Congress Theatre, Cwmbran.

In 2010 we took it to 12 theatres including Stockport Plaza, Medina Theatre Newport Isle of Wight, and four more performances at Jersey Opera House.

Finally, in 2012 we presented The Ugly Duckling at 15 more theatres including Grantham Guildhall, Middlesbrough Theatre, Swindon Arts Centre and 5 days at Lichfield Garrick. After that final tour ended, we sold the whole production, costumes, set, props, etc. to another Producer. Altogether we'd played Ugly Duckling at 172 theatre dates in total, and then sold it on. We can fairly say we made the most of that one! I have set out the full tour for you to see in Appendix 1.

2001 also saw our own very last performances of our puppet show. Although we'd given up touring to schools, we had continued appearing at a few small theatres ourselves in Derek Grant's Puppet Factory, or The Fruit Cake Mystery, at the same time as running the Pinocchio tour and The Ugly Duckling one. This was mainly to go all out to repay our debt to Steve and Patrick as quickly as possible. Our own final appearance on stage together was at the Civic Halls in Hoddesdon. In years to come, Michael would appear in our Bob Dylan music show performing some of Dylan's lyrics, and I would appear as interviewer in our "Evening with ..." celebrity shows.

Following our success with our variety shows, we wanted to expand into more variety and comedy. I looked in a showbusiness directory of available artistes and came across famous Irish comedian Jimmy Cricket. This one involved just ringing out of the blue to enquire his availability. We didn't have any connection with Jimmy or his son Dale Mulgrew who was now his agent.

It took a bit of persuading, and understandably so for they didn't know us from Adam, but eventually Jimmy agreed to do three shows for us as a trial. Once again, the fact that we were already successfully presenting The Bachelors Show on an ongoing basis was a great help. After we'd got going, we became good friends with Jimmy and his whole family. We got to know his lovely wife May, and his other son Frank. At the time, Frank was hoping to become a comedian like his famous father. As things have turned out, Frank has become a Catholic Priest, and I'm sure that's his real calling. No doubt, he can use his entertaining skills in the pulpit.

Jimmy and May's daughter Jamie worked for us, playing the title role in Little Red Riding Hood for our initial season of that one. She brought great charm, charisma and warmth to the role.

As regards the Jimmy Cricket Laughter Show, we played 30 theatres in all with Jimmy over several seasons which took in Skegness Embassy Theatre, Hastings White Rock Pavilion, Weymouth Pavilion (three times), Shrewsbury Music Hall, and the Scunthorpe Plowright Theatre. That was quite a memorable venue as we did three performances all in the same day. We did our children's production of Pinocchio in the afternoon (twice) and then gave the Pinocchio cast complimentary tickets to the comedy show in the evening with Jimmy Cricket and co.

Jimmy's warm Irish wit would have audiences in stitches. I would stand out in the foyer sometimes, talking to the theatre manager, and you could hear huge ripples of laughter coming from the auditorium.

Seamus and Paddy were on a flight from Dublin to Heathrow. The announcement came over the loudspeakers, "Ladies and gentlemen, we're pleased to assure you of the safety of this flight. We have four engines, so if one fails we'll still have another three. Our arrival time in London is 9.00 am.

After a little while, there came another announcement. Ladies and gentleman, I'm sorry to say that one of the engines has failed. Our arrival time will now be 10 o'clock.

A little later, there came another message. Ladies and gentlemen, I'm afraid the second engine has failed. Arrival time will now be 11 o'clock.

A bit later and ... Ladies and gentlemen, the third engine has failed. Arrival time is now 12 o'clock.

Paddy turned to Seamus and said I hope the fourth one doesn't fail or we shall be up here all day!

Support artistes for Jimmy varied. We'd come across a very talented lady by the name of Jan Brett one time when we were at the Grand Theatre, Wolverhampton. She'd won tv's Stars in Their Eyes as Alma Cogan and we offered her the chance to tour in a professional variety show singing the songs of Alma Cogan, Dusty Springfield and others. Apart from our shows, she was mostly working in clubs and Shearings hotels. Her talented husband Steve Rains joined her, singing songs of Jim Reeves which we quickly discovered were always a winner for British audiences.

Here's the review of our Jimmy Cricket Show from the Halstead Observer, which described it as a "rib-tickling evening, filled with brightness and happiness. David Conway's harmonica playing was great. He played fabulously, and we were entertained by Jan Brett. That was one of the best things. Each performer appeared a couple of times, ending with Jimmy's hilarious letter from his mammy. I loved every minute!"

In 2001, we also continued with the Humpty Dumpty Show, having adapted it a little into our own style. We played this at 16 theatres that year, at the same time as The Ugly Duckling tour was going around.

In the autumn, we wrote and created our own new production of Little Red Riding Hood along the lines of the shows we'd bought from Steve and Patrick.

We premiered it at the Alexandra Theatre Bognor Regis and then took it to 16 theatres during the autumn, including several in Northern Ireland and then a 26-performance Christmas engagement at the Courtyard Theatre on the edge of Belfast. We would successfully tour this show on and off right through until our very last children's theatre show on Michael's 50th birthday at the Ashcroft Theatre, Croydon in 2013.

Altogether, we presented Little Red Riding Hood in 247 performances at 167 theatres, from the Spa Theatre Bridlington to Bournemouth Pavilion, from Grimsby Auditorium to Jersey Opera House, from the Lowther Pavilion at Lytham St Annes to the Hackney Empire and many, many more in between.

<u>2002</u>

In the year when the Queen celebrated her Golden Jubilee, both Princess Margaret and the Queen Mother died. Who can forget the Queen Mother, on being asked about the high number of gay men working at Buckingham Palace, commenting "I'm not the only queen at the Palace you know".

By the end of the year, 50% of the population had internet access, and two more notable deaths included actor and pianist Dudley Moore and singer Lonnie Donegan. (A couple of years later, Michael and I presented a UK theatre tour of "The Lonnie Donegan Story" featuring his son Peter.)

We were approached by a local actor Raymond Sergeant. He'd read about us becoming producers and wondered if we'd like to produce a theatre tour of his one-man show Two Victorian Tales. He'd put together a two-part performance featuring a ghost story by Thomas Hardy and The Signalman by Charles Dickens. We readily agreed and a deal was struck.

Little did we know that the Dickens portion of his show was a foretaste of what was to come a few years later! We got 16 theatres to book the show and thereby took Raymond to Margate Theatre Royal, Porthcawl Grand Pavilion, Hartlepool Town Hall and thirteen others. Sadly, Raymond passed away at a very early age. He was a lovely man and a fine actor.

Another new departure for us in 2002 was a tour with Sheridan Morley. His management approached us and asked if we'd like to produce an evening of Noel Coward songs and anecdotes featuring Sheridan and an accompanist on piano. It was to be called A Talent to Amuse, which some readers will know is a line from one of Noel's songs – If Love Were All. This again was a great success and we ran these Noel Coward shows at the same time as our tours of Little Red Riding Hood, The Ugly Duckling, and Humpty Dumpty.

What sage advice Noel Coward gave!

"Work hard, do the best you can, don't ever lose faith in yourself and take no notice of what other people say about you."

"Conceit is an outward manifestation of inferiority."

"You will know you're old when you cease to be amazed."

"People are wrong when they say opera is not what it used to be. It IS what it used to be. That's what's wrong with it."

We took Sheridan Morley and the songs of Noel Coward to Derby Guildhall, Swindon Arts Centre, and The Mill at Sonning. We also put him on locally at our Tivoli Theatre in Wimborne. Here's the review of that one, from the Bournemouth Daily Echo.

"I had high hopes for this evening, and it surpassed all my expectations. Mr Morley knew Coward well, and it was blissful to listen to him chatting with such genuine warmth and such an easy manner – not a script in sight – about the man known so appropriately as The Master. As if that wasn't enough, the anecdotes were interspersed with music from the outstandingly talented Michael Law at the piano."

Our Noel Coward show was another way of increasing our range, so to speak. We were beginning to be seen in the business as quite versatile producers, and we were learning which venues were suitable for which kind of show. Small to medium theatres and arts centres were ideal for Two Victorian Tales and A Talent to Amuse, while bigger seaside and municipal theatres were taking our children's offerings which were filling quite big houses in those days.

It was just that we now had five tours on the go, all in the same year, but that wasn't going to be all for 2002.

When we were at a Water Rats event in London earlier in the year, we'd met Melvyn Hayes. He'd started out with Cliff Richard in The Young Ones and Summer Holiday, and had had a good run in It Ain't Half Hot Mum! He'd told us that he'd been developing a stand-up comedy act, and in fact we'd seen him going down a storm with this, performing to his peers at the Water Rats. Michael had the idea of putting him in a show along with two others we'd recently met – The Krankies! What lovely people. Melvyn was a perfect gentleman to work with, and Ian and Jeanette were so friendly to us. Not only that, but great talents. Have you seen their "cod" vent act with Wee Jimmy on Ian's knee?

Michael put the show together with the two comedy acts and other support artistes and we took them to seaside venues from Torquay to Morecambe and many more in between. When we played Torquay, the Krankies invited Melvyn and ourselves to their home and cooked us a lovely dinner late at night after the show. Michael called the show It Ain't Half Fun Mum, after Melvyn's famous television series, and it certainly was fun working with those funny people!

Talking of the seaside reminds me that our Jimmy Cricket shows were also continuing in 2002. We played the Jimmy Cricket Laughter Show that year at Ilfracombe, Weymouth, Skegness, Worthing and other resorts.

My GP doubled my blood pressure pills.

When we were appearing at Weymouth with our Jimmy Cricket show, we went over the road from the theatre to a fish and chip shop in between the rehearsal and the show. Michael's mobile phone rang and we discovered that it was his Aunt Mary, his mother's sister. We hadn't heard from any of Michael's family since the exchange of letters in

1996. She was ringing to say that Michael's sister Shelagh wanted to be in touch with us again. Much as this was very good news to put it mildly, it was very traumatic to suddenly be confronted with this just before doing a public performance at a big theatre.

We coped with the evening and the show went exceptionally well, with the big audience in absolute stitches over Jimmy's humour plus a good reception for all our supporting cast.

To cut a long story short, we were so pleased to be in touch with Shelagh again. We didn't know she had married (Gary) and they had a son, Max. We started to see quite a lot of them, especially when they came to Dorset on holiday, travelling from their home in Peterborough.

This is not the place to relate all the details of the relationship between us and Shelagh's family, but suffice to say it was extremely emotional and not at all easy. We are close to Shelagh now, as I write in 2020, but sadly she has divorced and is struggling with various issues of her own as well as bringing up Max who unbelievably is now 19.

Michael's brother Stephen continues to keep away from the rest of the family. He is living in Glasgow, where he has been working in customer relations, and we did have one very difficult meeting with him at a hotel in Hook, Hampshire. It was clear from that encounter that he would rather go his own way, apart from the rest of us.

Everyone seemed to be doing tribute shows. With a dearth of new artistes available for medium-scale touring, the obvious thing was to present shows harking back to the golden days of the sixties and seventies. The number one tribute show was Abba. At one time, there were eight different Abba shows on the road!

With the idea of tributes in my head, I tried to think of something we could do that hadn't already been done. Jimmy Cricket's genial humour was going down well, as was the comedy of our funny lady Dottie Wayne. What about a tribute to Joyce Grenfell? She'd been a huge name with her original take on British life as it once was. Her monologues featured subjects like the Women's Institute, a day at the funfair, and of course her famous nursery school routine "George! Don't do that!"

After much negotiation, I managed to acquire the professional rights to 20 of her sketches for presentation at theatres in the UK, on the proviso that we perform the sketches only and did not include any biographical details about Joyce. This was because Maureen Lipman had been presenting Re- Joyce! in the West End to great acclaim, and that was basically the story of the famous lady including some of her sketches on the way through.

The rights were quite expensive, but it was a gamble we were prepared to take. Money was coming in from our other shows all the time.

We auditioned for the part of Joyce and engaged a young actress Maria Gibbs who'd appeared in some of our children's shows. She was more than capable and performed as Joyce for us at 82 theatres altogether, along with a pianist and company stage manager. We opened at Doncaster Civic and found that we were playing to full or nearly full houses everywhere. Soon theatres were falling over themselves to get a Best of Joyce Grenfell date from us and the whole thing was an amazing success.

By this time, we'd made friends with pianist Bobby Crush and he came to our Joyce Grenfell show at Potters Bar where I got Maria to introduce him to the audience in the finale.

In Appendix 3, I've put a review of our Joyce Grenfell Show from the local paper in Lichfield re our performance at the Garrick Theatre there.

Before I leave the subject of Joyce Grenfell, I have to tell you that somebody in the audience died during our performance at Leicester. My cousin Rosemary and her husband John who live in Leicester were there, and it was a full house. When the interval came, we all made our way to the bar. One lady remained in the auditorium, sitting particularly still! Upon examination, concerns were raised and the St John Ambulance volunteers, who were always in attendance wherever we went, decided an ambulance should be called. To cut a long story short, the lady had passed away, and instead of her being taken to hospital, her body had to be carried out. All this caused the interval to last

55 minutes instead of the allotted 20, after which our performer Maria Gibbs had to start the second half, attempting to play comedy!

That wasn't all we did in 2002. Our children's shows were proving a great success, but we'd done several tours of the ones we'd bought from Stephen and Patrick. Even Red Riding Hood had done the rounds a few times, so once again we needed something new!

I realised that nobody was touring Goldilocks and the Three Bears. It was a rarely performed pantomime subject, but a popular children's story and we decided to go for it. We had a new set made and collected together all the necessary props and costumes. Michael wrote a strong script and we kept to the traditional panto format, setting it in the circus.

Goldilocks runs the circus with her father the Ringmaster. Business is struggling and they need a new act. Along come three very talented bears who can sing, dance and tell jokes. Just when business is booming again for Goldilocks, Baron Von Lederhosen, the wicked owner of a rival circus, tricks Goldi and kidnaps the bears so that he can put them in HIS show.

Goldi and the Ringmaster need to trick the Baron in order to free the bears. This they finally do, with the help of Russell the Crow and, in a happy ending, the wicked Baron is sent away from Circusland, never to return.

We featured some great songs from the musical Barnum, engaged a good choreographer who'd worked for us before, and Michael directed the rehearsals at a theatre in west London.

I was there for the dress rehearsal, and then waved them all off in the van to start the long tour Shirley had booked.

As soon as the tour started, we could see this one was going to be a winner. We had full houses everywhere, and audiences were walking out into the foyer singing the praises of our talented cast.

The best memory of Goldilocks is when I turned up to our show at the New Theatre, Hull. It seats 1600, and every single one of the 1600 seats had been sold!

"I'll just stand at the back," I said, but this wasn't allowed even though I was the producer of the show. Elf'n'Safety.

In the end, they gave me the royal box, where I sat all alone, gazing down on my very short-lasting kingdom! I resisted the temptation to regally wave.

We played 175 theatres altogether with Goldilocks between 2002 and 2011. Several come to mind, such as Bradford St George's Hall, Bournemouth Pavilion, Antrim Arts Theatre, and the Prince of Wales Theatre, Cannock.

We had this letter from the manager of the theatre at Limavady in Northern Ireland ...

"I am writing to express my delight at the outstanding presentation of Goldilocks and the Three Bears. The cast were simply fantastic, holding the audience spellbound and fully engulphed in the story, action and music. Please convey to the cast my appreciation for such an amazing delivery and creation of such an electric atmosphere, drawing the constant attention of the participative audiences. I look forward to welcoming you back."

Another more amusing memory of our Goldilocks tour is from when we were playing the Floral Pavilion, New Brighton on the Wirral. I stood by the doors as the full house started to leave. One elderly gentleman was making very slow progress as he exited the auditorium, hobbling with a stick. Just to cheer things along as he was holding a lot of people up, I said "Have you enjoyed the show?", fishing for praise I'm afraid.

He replied "I preferred the second half".

"Why's that?" I asked, in innocence.

"Because it was shorter!"

<u>2003</u>

In the largest ever demonstration in the UK so far, two million people protested against the Iraq War. In London, the congestion charge was introduced, and in Birmingham the Bull Ring shopping centre was expanded. Nearby, and circling Birmingham to the north east, the first toll motorway was also opened.

Rolling Stone Mick Jagger was knighted, and Rowan Williams became Archbishop of Canterbury. A decade later, Michael and I heard him speak at Church House near

Westminster Abbey, and I went to his evening of poetry at Theatr Brycheiniog in mid Wales, which happened to be on the night before one of our own shows there. I thought he was a great speaker.

This was the year we lost Bee Gee Maurice Gibb, Dame Thora Hird, and the great American comedian Bob Hope, who was in fact British, having been born at Eltham, in Greater London. He managed to just reach 100, outliving his close friend George Burns by a year. The two of them had always planned to play the London Palladium together to mark their 100th birthdays but they didn't quite make it.

Ten years earlier, Michael and I had been to Bob Hope's 90th birthday at the London Palladium where one of his guest stars was Danny la Rue. We would never have guessed at the time that we would go on to produce The Danny la Rue Show ourselves.

At 90 years old, Bob Hope was a revelation, and a text book example of how to perform comedy on a huge stage in a prestigious theatre – the most prestigious theatre in the world, as it happened.

From the moment he walked on to his famous theme tune Thanks for the Memory, he held the audience in the palm of his hand. Although British by birth, his style was the traditional American wise-crack one-liners.

"When I began, TV Guide had one page."

"I gotta tell you, on my ninetieth birthday, if I had my life to live over again, I wouldn't have the time."

His devoted wife Dolores also made an appearance and sang a duet with him.

"Dolores is always asking me, when you go, where do you want to be buried? In the cemetery at Palm Springs, or here in our own plot? I say, surprise me!"

As I write in 2020, we have just lost legendary comedy writer Carl Reiner, creator of The Dick Van Dyke Show, who is credited for having thought of George Burns' famous line. "When I wake up, I get the papers and I read the obituaries. If I'm not in them, I have breakfast."

Thinking of obituaries, 2003 was the year my father died at the age of 89. This was a major event. He'd had quite a few years living by himself at 11 Shirley Avenue, using just the downstairs part of the house as a bungalow. Eventually he said he'd really like someone else to look after him and decided to go into a home, the same one that his mother Bess, my Grandma Webb, had stayed in through her last years. It was just along the road at the other end of Shirley Avenue.

Peter and I would often visit, and Michael and I would do the same. He introduced Michael to the ladies on the staff saying "this is my son's partner and he is like another son to me". He became very fond of Michael as Michael was of him. Contrast that remark with my father's earlier pronouncements. What progress.

Eventually, my father had to move from the rest home in Shirley Avenue to a proper nursing home at Rownhams. It was there that he passed away. He was certainly ailing, but we hadn't yet expected the end to come.

One fateful day, Peter and I visited together. We walked along the corridor to his room and opened the door. Can you believe that the staff had not told us that our father had died?

We were confronted with the sight of his body in the armchair, his head fallen back, his mouth open. It didn't take a moment to decide he was dead. Peter was very capable as always, while I was hugely distressed.

Once again, we two brothers did everything together, making all the arrangements, getting probate, etc. One of the most distressing events of my life so far was attending my father's funeral. Suffice to say I was traumatised.

Auntie Marjorie died. I was very moved at her funeral. I couldn't believe how her family had put together a wonderful tribute to her and delivered it themselves. I remember thinking I just wouldn't have been able to stand there and say it all without breaking down. I also remember wishing she could have got to know Michael as I think we'd have all got on very well together. She'd invited us both to lunch at her house in Ealing and it had been a very nice occasion. However, I'd felt so nervous about bringing my male partner to see her that I just couldn't face taking him there again. It was a one-off as they say, and now any further meetings are not to be.

Our children's shows and pantomimes continued, with several tours running at the same time. Out of the blue, we were approached by the Britannia Pier Theatre at Great Yarmouth, asking if we could put together a one-off variety night for them with a star top of the bill. Somebody suggested Vince Hill, a stylish singer with real class and presence on stage. Vince invited us to his home near Henley on Thames and showed us his huge library of sheet music. Every standard you could possibly think of, all filed along with copies of his hit singles and albums. I told him what we had in mind and thereby began a long association which saw him touring for us for five years. We played the seaside with Vince including dates at Ilfracombe, Torquay, Eastbourne, Clacton and Blackpool. Every show featured his No 1 hit Edelweiss plus Roses of Picardy and many others. He would open with Elton John's I'm Still Standing, going into I Love Being Here with You by Peggy Lee. I think it was the Peggy Lee song that sealed our relationship on our first visit to Vince's home. He was running past me the songs he was thinking of singing in his act and mentioned I Love Being Here with You as an opener. "Oh yes," I said. "Peggy Lee." He hadn't mentioned that she was the composer and was astounded that I knew.

Instead of replying to me, he called out of the door of his office into the kitchen. "Annie! Derek knows it's by Peggy Lee!"

His wife Annie always accompanied him and she was in the wings each night just out of view behind the curtain. It was clear that he sang all his love songs to her. They were a devoted couple.

Vince and Annie invited us again to their house at Shiplake near Henley on Thames and took us out for a picnic on their boat. Another time they gave us their tickets to the Members' Enclosure at Henley Regatta. When we told them about our Civil Partnership in 2007, they insisted on celebrating with us with champagne at their village pub.

As we got to know them, Vince told us how pleased he was to be working for producers who were actually interested in the shows they were producing. Hence the initial delight about my knowledge of his favourite Peggy Lee song.

This was the year we decided to expand our comedy shows. We'd had success with funny man Jimmy Cricket, and on that basis decided to produce a bigger show with two more comics joining him. We engaged Don Maclean and Bernie Clifton (with his ostrich – remember?)

I've written already about Don Maclean. He had been a star of Crackerjack on tv and had presented Good Morning Sunday on BBC Radio 2 for the last 11 years. His rapid quick-fire gags contrasted well with Jimmy's inoffensive charm, and Bernie Clifton would bring zany visual humour to the proceedings. I got the three of them to do an opening number together "We Want to Say Hello!" and then they each had their own spot. Jimmy oversaw a sketch routine at the beginning of the second half which featured all three of them.

Spencer K Gibbins, who'd so skilfully stage managed our Joyce Grenfell tour, was on board once again to oversee the tour for us. Overall, another 23 theatres took our Funny Guys show including the Spa Pavilion at Felixstowe, where we opened, the Southport Theatre, York Grand Opera House, Swansea Grand Theatre, and Rhyl Pavilion.

Don Maclean would say things like "I was at the supermarket, and there was an old man on his own in front of me. He bought a little tin of butter beans, an apple, and an individual pork pie. The check-out girl said 'You're a single gentleman, aren't you!' 'How could you tell?' he said. 'Cos you're really ugly.'"

Irish comedian Jimmy Cricket would play the part of a simpleton, a very charming character.

"My neighbour came round. He said, how many rolls of wallpaper did you take to do your front room? I said ten. He was back the next week. He said, I've got two rolls left over! I said, so have I".

"I went to the railway station. I said, can I have a return ticket. The clerk said, where to? I said, back here!"

Remember Jimmy's 'letter from me mammy'? This is the kind of thing ...

"Dear Son, Just a line to let you know we're still here. I'm writing slowly as I know you can't read fast. Your father has a lovely new job. He has 500 men under him. He cuts the grass at the cemetery.

Your sister Mary had a baby this morning, but I haven't found out if it's a boy or a girl, so I don't know if you're an aunt or an uncle.

Your uncle Patrick drowned las week in a vat of whisky at the Dublin Brewery. His workmates tried to save him but he fought them off bravely. They cremated him and it took three days to put out the fire.

I went to the doctor on Thursday and your father came with me. The doctor put a tube in my mouth and told me not to talk for ten minutes. Your father offered to buy it from him.

We're trying to save money so we only turn on the electric clock when we want to know the time.

I'm returning the jacket you left behind in a separate parcel. I cut the buttons off to save the weight. You'll find them in the top pocket.

Your loving Mother.

PS I was going to send you a ten pound note for your birthday, but I'd already sealed the envelope."

Unfortunately, Bernie Clifton was taken ill and he, his ostrich, and gigantic inflatable sausage, had to leave the tour. We replaced him with Mel Harvey for some of the dates, and Steve Barclay for the rest. These were both talented artistes but they weren't "names" and business suffered a bit.

<u>2004</u>

Fathers4Justice staged a protest at Prime Minister's Questions and at Buckingham Palace over the thousands of children who are denied access to their fathers. In local elections, Labour started to lose numerous seats. Huge numbers of people were killed in the Indian Ocean tsunami, and here, the Diana Memorial Fountain was opened.

Openly gay cleric Jeffrey John was installed as Dean of St Albans. 15 years later, Michael and I heard him give a passionate talk at a church in Salisbury attended by around 200 people, highlighting the plight of gay Christians and their treatment.

Alan Hollinghurst's novel "The Line of Beauty" was published.

Sir Peter Ustinov passed away. The Agatha Christie films in which he so marvellously portrays Hercule Poirot are some of our favourites, and we have watched them numerous times – "Evil Under the Sun", "Death on the Nile", "Thirteen at Dinner", "Dead Man's Folly", "Appointment with Death", etc. We also have his "Audience With..." television programme from 1988.

Daughter of Gloria Hunniford, Caron Keating sadly died at the early age of 42. When we started our celebrity "Evening With ..." tours, we were approached by Gloria's agent to discuss the possibility of her touring for us. I had two very pleasant meetings with the agent, but it wasn't to be for a number of reasons.

Anthony Buckeridge, author of the Jennings books I'd enjoyed as a boy, died, as did actress Molly Weir. We all remember her cheerful "Arden Hoose" when answering the phone for Dr Cameron. Journalist Lynda Lee Potter, and steeplejack Fred Dibnah also passed away. Lynda lived just along from the Springfield Country House Hotel at Wareham, which is one of our favourite haunts for morning coffee. Fred Dibnah's wife Sheila approached us after her husband's death. She had put together a film evening and talk about his exploits and wanted to tour it to theatres. I met her in Blackpool, but, like the Gloria Hunniford idea, I wasn't able to run with it. We were often approached by people with ideas for shows but most of them were just not viable, interesting though they may have been.

This was the year of our big Summer Season in Clacton. We'd done quite a few shows there at the West Cliff Theatre, and they'd all gone well. Out of the blue, they approached us to ask if we'd like to produce their forthcoming Summer Season. This was 8 weeks of shows, four shows a week Wednesday to Saturday. I went over to meet the team, and a deal was struck. The council would "buy out" the whole season of 32 shows on a guarantee. All we had to do was to find the performers and put together the whole thing. The problem was they wanted four different shows each week. Normally, a summer season would consist of the same production running all the time. In the end we booked Joan

Regan and supporting artistes on Wednesdays, Vince Hill and a different line up on Thursdays, Maggie Moone and yet more support acts on Fridays, and Stan Stennett and co on Saturdays.

Clacton was a long way away! We kept having to drive over there, all the way up the M3, all the way round the M25, and then all the way out along the A12 to the Essex coast. We engaged Tony Smart as our company manager there to oversee the whole run and liaise with the different casts and the theatre technicians and management. He was a wonderful asset, as he'd been on Pinocchio.

I was quite inexperienced when it came to summer season contracts. It was fine that the council were paying for the whole thing, and the amount I'd negotiated made us a reasonable profit on the run but it was Stan Stennett who asked me "Have you got an option?" I didn't know what he meant. Stan was an astute businessman as well as a talented and versatile performer. In his time, he'd staged numerous pantomime seasons as producer and star, and had also managed and run the Roses Theatre at Tewkesbury. It was during Stan's tenure there that Eric Morecambe died. Stan had booked the legendary comedian to talk about his life in showbusiness. The same end befell Eric as did Tommy Cooper. He died on stage – or only just off.

To go back to the idea of an option, this meant we would have the opportunity to do another one or two seasons if we so wished, all on the same terms. I'd not thought of anything like that.

As it turned out, we wouldn't have wanted to repeat the experience. All our artistes were a delight to work with, and Tony Smart was the ideal company manager, but there were a number of local problems that would have made us turn down the chance to return.

In addition to the 8 week summer season, we also did a few one-off variety shows at Clacton that year, including one with a big cast topped by Bert Weedon, the legendary guitarist. He brought in a full house and was clearly loved by the audience who queued up in droves to get his autograph after the show. Guitarists like Eric Clapton and Brian May always credit Bert Weedon as their mentor.

This was quite a year! Separate to our season at Clacton, we also toured Danny la Rue to 24 big theatres all over England.

We opened our big Danny la Rue show at Camberley Theatre, went on to Margate Winter Gardens, played three days at the Kenneth More, Ilford before setting off all round the country, ending up at Lichfield Garrick. Working with Danny was quite something.

We'd engaged an experienced tour booker Richard Clark who'd booked our various comedy shows into theatres, and I'd confided in him that it was so difficult having to keep trying to think of something new to offer. He'd said to me "If you could get Danny la Rue, the world would beat a path to your door."

As it happened, David and Pauline Conway, the musical act who'd appeared in some of our variety shows, had worked a lot with Danny. I mentioned all this to David and he told me Danny was currently looking for another producer!

"Meant to be!"

Danny lived in Southampton at Bassett, not far from my brother and his family. David rang Danny, and within a few hours, Danny invited us over to meet him at home. Danny La Rue was known in the business for his HUGE ego. Danny must surely have invented the concept of self-belief, for he exuded it in everything he said and did.

He had a housekeeper who welcomed us in. Once we were seated in the lounge, Danny made his entrance. He offered us coffee, and when the housekeeper went out to the kitchen to get it, he told us "She adores me!"

Later, after he'd been working for us a while, I remember he had a problem with a wisdom tooth. He said he was going to the dentist the next day, adding "My dentist adores me".

On that first meeting, Danny asked me who else had worked for us in terms of "star" names. I reeled off as many as I could think of and when I'd finished he said "I am worth all of those put together".

In a way it was true, but Danny wasn't one given to modesty. He could command a stage and hold an audience spellbound – and he knew it! And he would tell you so.

He toured with a little shrine to the Virgin Mary. A little statue with a pictorial surround, he would place it in front of him in his dressing room wherever we went. When I enquired about it, he said "That's my lovely Mary. She talks to me".

Our Danny la Rue show was a big production, and it did big business. After the tour was over, Danny wanted to do more but, again due to something else I hadn't so far learned, he wanted a higher fee for the next tour. I should have agreed that the fee was the same for subsequent tours, particularly as we discovered we were paying him £250 per performance MORE than his previous producer had done. So much for my negotiating skills!

Anyway, we had terrific response to the tour, including this from the manager of the Garrick Theatre, Lichfield.

"Our audience loved the show so much they gave it a standing ovation."

That year, we also toured a show we called The Magic of Judy Garland, featuring one of the Nolan Sisters, Denise, and a big orchestra which we decided to call The Rainbow Concert Orchestra. 22 theatres in all booked that one, including the Gala Theatre Durham, The Grand Theatre at Blackpool and the Royal Hippodrome, Eastbourne. If you work in professional showbusiness, you work in the whole country as it could be anywhere at all that you get your bookings.

We needed a pantomime for the Christmas season as we were booked once again in Belfast for 26 performances. Looking back, Dick Whittington was not a very good choice. To be honest, we struggled to do it in a small scale kind of way, both in terms of the set and script. In the end we did play it for 56 days in all through the winter, including our last visit to the Hackney Empire and 20 dates in Northern Ireland, but we never presented that title again. Not our proudest moment.

<u>2005</u>

The BBC broadcast "Jerry Springer – The Opera", despite having received 45 thousand complaints. Conservative MP Robert Jackson defected and joined the Labour Party. At the General Election, Labour won again but with a much reduced majority. The Lib Dems gained 62 MPs.

John Sentamu became the first black man to be made Archbishop of York.

52 were killed and a further 700 injured in a series of terrorist bomb attacks on London Transport. The IRA announced an end to its armed campaign, promising to concentrate only on politics in the future.

The Civil Partnership Act became law, allowing same-sex couples to form an alliance similar to a marriage with many of the same rights.

Former Prime Ministers James Callaghan and Edward Heath both died, as did Sir John Mills. His daughter Hayley had always been one of my favourite actresses, my two top films of hers being "The Moon Spinners" with Sheila Hancock and John le Mesurier, and "Appointment with Death" with Peter Ustinov as Hercule Poirot. We saw her in pantomime in Richmond when she played Fairy Godmother quite charmingly, with her scripted lines making numerous references to "The Parent Trap", "Pollyanna" etc.

2005 saw us start to tour Tenorissimo! They were billed as "three tenors in concert", and were absolutely fabulous, as they say. The three guys sang beautifully, and their act was spiced with light, amusing banter and audience participation. In a classic example of how things are in showbusiness, we opened at an Arts Centre in Worcestershire. The house was full, and before the show started lots of people were coming into the box office trying to get tickets, only to be turned away. The box office staff told me they could have sold at least fifty more seats. At the end of the show, the audience all gave a standing ovation for our wonderful performers. I stood in the foyer as the audience left, and people were asking me when we'd be coming back again.

Here's the reality check. No matter how many times Michael phoned, the theatre NEVER booked that show again. We reckoned they'd made at least £1000 profit on the performance, not bad for a small arts centre, plus all their bar sales and catering. But, as I intimated, here's the reality of the situation. There are so many shows being offered to small/medium venues that they are always unable to fit everything into their schedule. You need to keep coming up with something new.

"What are you offering NEXT year?" Have I mentioned that before?

As far as Tenorissimo were concerned, we didn't actually need to go back to that Worcestershire Arts Centre as we took the guys all over the UK, everywhere from the Barrington Theatre near home in Ferndown to Retford Majestic Theatre and right up to the Macrobert Arts Centre in Stirling.

In 2005 we took our Frankie Howerd "Titter Ye Not!" show out on the road again, starring the multi-talented Paul Harris. We did it as a one-man show this time, and everyone said he was uncanny in his likeness to the late comedian.

Stan Stennett, who'd been such a pleasure to work with at Clacton approached us with a wartime show he'd put together with Johnny Tudor from tv's Gavin and Stacey. It was a good show, and the artistes were all lovely, but it didn't do a lot of business. We got just three theatres to take it. We'd return to the wartime theme with a little more success, however, in 2013 with Hits from the Blitz.

Our Little Red Riding Hood tour was still continuing, playing big theatres everywhere. We had engaged a young lady to manage the tour and drive the van, but while they were in Jersey at the Opera House she became ill. We met the company when they returned to Poole on the ferry and then Michael said he'd really have to take over from her. We wished her a speedy recovery and, in a flash, Michael had become Company Stage Manager. Once again, he'd brought about one of the big changes in our life.

He turned out to be very good at it, keeping all the cast's egos at bay! His first date as CSM was at Weymouth Pavilion, where everything went swimmingly.

When the Red Riding Hood tour ended, we decided it would be good for him to do a lot more company managing in the future, and he went to London to learn professional stage lighting and sound. This would stand us in good stead as things progressed.

I've never really been a "joiner" as they say. I'm not much for groups and societies. Someone, however, suggested it would be good for our networking, etc. if I joined the Concert Artistes' Association. This would link us with all sorts of agents, actors, singers, etc. which would be a real help to our future shows.

Comedienne Dotty Wayne proposed me, and suggested Danny La Rue to second the proposal. She said she'd ring him to arrange things.

The next thing we knew, we had Danny La Rue on the phone. Shirley never found him easy to speak to, and this conversation was no different. He said to her, "I think there's been a mistake".

"What sort of a mistake, Danny?"

"Well, I understand Derek is going to join the CAA, and I'm to second the proposal."

"Yes, that's right. Dottie Wayne is proposing him."

"THAT'S the mistake! I am Danny La Rue! I never SECOND anything!"

There's good and bad in everyone, as we all know only too well, and there was a lot of good in Danny. When his final dates with us ended, he gave us a quote that said "Where you see on a poster 'Derek Grant presents' you know you will see quality". He told us we could use it wherever we liked, which was certainly a great help.

The amount of work we were able to offer Shirley was reducing, and she needed to move on. She had been enormously helpful in many ways. She and her husband Sandy were tremendously interested in all our exploits, and remain so, as we do in theirs. We see them often, and enjoy catching up with our respective news.

Stage Seven:
Diversification and Change.

In which we move to West Moors, buy ANOTHER company, and enter a Civil Partnership together.

<u>2006</u>

Charles Kennedy resigned as Leader of the Liberal Democrats, citing a drink problem, and The Queen celebrated her 80th birthday.

Freddie and the Dreamers singer Freddie Garrity died, along with disc jockey Alan Freeman. ("Greetings Pop Pickers!" "All right? Stay bright!") At this time we'd started being invited to showbusiness parties at Brinsworth House at Twickenham, which is a rest home for the profession. It was quite moving to have seen him there as one of the residents, sadly quite decrepit.

Actor Alec Bregonzi died. He had appeared in 22 of the "Hancock's Half Hours", many of the Two Ronnies shows, and numerous other comedies and films, always as a support artiste, not as a "star". I had met him at a party in London, and had visited his flat at Wandsworth a few times.

A well-respected producer and impresario, Richard Gill approached us to say he was retiring and would like to sell several of his stunning and highly successful productions.

Richard had founded the famous, award-winning Polka Theatre for Children at Wimbledon and had gone on to create the touring Parasol Theatre Company. We had several meetings with Richard and his wife Liz, and after many negotiations, we bought The Snow Queen, Aladdin, and Pinocchio, lock stock and barrel. We acquired the rights to Richard's very literary scripts, along with the beautiful sets, props and costumes, in effect buying out the majority of his company.

Our first outing with our newly-acquired properties was with Hans Christian Andersen's The Snow Queen. The whole show looked gorgeous, and the writing was first class. We auditioned in London for a cast of six actors and a Company Manager to take the show around the country, and we opened the tour at the Forum Theatre, Billingham. Altogether we toured The Snow Queen three times, with a different cast each time. Only 33 theatres booked it in all, but with most engagements being for several days or even a week rather than our usual one-nighters, it was a huge success taking in theatres everywhere from Wrexham to Croydon, and from Bournemouth Pavilion to the Broadway Theatre, Peterborough.

Whenever we played Peterborough, Michael's sister Shelagh would come to the show, usually bringing her son Max. It was always lovely to see them both and to have their support.

For our third Snow Queen tour, we decided to engage a "name" for the title role. Just as we were thinking about this,

Jane Rossington, star of Crossroads, appeared on a television chat show. It was clear how much she was loved by the audience and this, combined with the fact that we'd been booked for the week at a leading Midlands theatre, made us feel she would be ideal. Crossroads was a Midlands serial, shown daily on ATV for around 20 years.

We approached Jane's agent and a deal was done. I have to say Jane was one of the nicest people who ever worked for us, and she brought people in to see her wherever we went, signing programmes and autographs with grace and charm. She really moved the show up quite a bit. Definitely next level, as they say nowadays.

As well as our new tour of The Snow Queen, our Ugly Duckling tour was also continuing. For this year's version, Michael was the full-time Company Manager from the start. After his success the previous year with taking over Little Red Riding Hood, and after the work he'd put in learning stage lighting and sound, we decided he would direct and rehearse the whole production this time. We hired a room at a theatre near Uxbridge where we held auditions for the various parts, and then rehearsed the whole thing there for a week.

The first date on the tour was at Luton Library Theatre, where Michael proved his versatility once again!

Another great advantage of Michael being the Company Manager was the fact that he was in control of the merchandising and programme selling. On one of our previous tours, we'd had £3000 programme money stolen from us by the CSM. This we had to just "write off", as there was no way we could afford to start legal proceedings. Such is "justice". Now Michael held the purse strings.

After we'd done so well with Joyce Grenfell, we hit on the idea of Flanders and Swann, which seemed to be in a similar vein. The songs were available under a standard royalty agreement and didn't require a special licence like the Joyce material. We engaged veteran comedian Gordon Peters and our favourite musical director David Carter. They made a most appealing double act but theatres weren't so keen on the concept, and in the event only 5 theatres booked it.

A daughter, Lexie was born to Rachel and Sean in November, becoming my brother Peter and his wife Barbara's third grandchild, and my great-niece.

In Wimborne, cousin Kathleen died. She had been in a "home" for her last years since her sisters Muriel and Ena had passed away. An amazing connection with Kathleen was that in her working life, she had been seamstress at the Royal Norfolk Hotel on Richmond Hill in Bournemouth. When Kathleen retired, Michael's mother Gina, took up that same position until her own retirement!

<u>2007</u>

Gordon Brown became Prime Minister, replacing Tony Blair.

New rules prohibited businesses from discriminating against homosexuals. In other words, until then they had been legally ALLOWED to discriminate against Michael and me!

The Climate Change Bill made mandatory a 60% reduction in carbon emissions by 2050, and widespread heavy flooding caused devastation in a sign of things to come.

Unpleasant comedian Bernard Manning died, along with "Are You Being Served?" actor John Inman, and Hollywood actress Deborah Kerr. Her singing voice had been dubbed in "The King and I" by versatile vocalist Marni Nixon whose voice was regularly used for actresses who appeared in musicals but couldn't sing! Audrey Hepburn in "My Fair Lady" was another one of many dubbed by Marni.

Sheridan Morley also passed away. You may recall he had toured for us in our production of "A Talent to Amuse", an evening of the songs and wit of Noel Coward.

One time, when we were with Sheridan in the dressing room somewhere, I referred to the Sherman Brothers' musical Chitty Chitty Bang Bang which had just opened in the West End, and asked what he'd thought of it. "It's just pap, darling," he replied.

Which reminds me, in all my years in the theatre, I never once managed to call anyone "darling"!

Once again, we moved house. We'd been treated terribly by the neighbours at Stapehill, and we really wanted to get away from there. On one occasion, the man next door to us, who clearly felt we shouldn't be together, shouted at us "Queer boys, I'll burn your house down."

I think I've already intimated I'm of a very nervous disposition. Incidents like that may help to explain why.

Another reason for us wanting to move was that we were paying £300 a month to rent a storage room at a farm near Colehill for our scenery and costumes. If we could store all that at home, it would be worth buying a bigger house. We found a lovely house at West Moors in a quiet cul-de-sac, and decided we loved West Moors in general and the house in particular! There was room in the garden to have a big outbuilding built which, together with the big double garage and several of the bedrooms, then housed everything and saved us the £3600 a year rent at Colehill.

What with the move, and still producing all our on-going theatre tours, this was quite a year as on the 19th June, Michael and I entered a Civil Partnership. It was held at the Registry Office in Ferndown, and 32 friends and family attended what was a wonderful, joyous occasion. Michael and I both gave speeches, as did Shirley and Sandy. Sandy took some lovely photos, and the main one of the two of us together on the lawn outside the Registry Office is one of our most treasured possessions.

And then there were the rings! I've said before how much we love North Wales and the Cambrian Coast area in particular. There was a little gold mine at Bontddu, just north west of Dolgellau, high above the Mawddach Estuary. Gold from there is very rare and there were only a few wedding rings made there. It's now closed. The Queen Mother's came from Bontddu mine, as did Camilla's – and ours!! It's called Clogau Gold.

We had a lunch after the ceremony at the pub in our village of West Moors. The landlady, Jill, had always been very friendly to us, and we arrived to find she'd decked out the whole bar and lounge with rainbow flags and balloons!

Many people at that time (less so now) strongly felt that people like us shouldn't be allowed to be married, even though it was called something different. We kept it simple, inviting close friends and just a few family representatives. Of these I had six – my brother Peter and sister-in-law Barbara, plus two cousins on my mother's side Rosemary and Jennifer, and two cousins on my father's side John and Wendy. Michael had just one, his sister Shelagh. My friend Alun travelled from Devon to be with us.

An interesting element is that the relationships created by a Civil Partnership are the same as for a marriage. For example, Shelagh became my sister-in-law, Michael became Barbara's brother-in-law. Max is now my nephew. Michael is Rachel and Nina's uncle. We are officially married now in any case, but the legal relationships have existed since the date of our Civil Partnership.

When we looked at the photos later, we noticed that my brother Peter was standing strangely, looking round sideways with his head down. Unknown to us all at the time, this was the first sign of the Parkinsons Disease which was to eventually take his life 12 years later, after a long and devastating decline.

The following day we set off on "honeymoon" by Eurostar to Brussels, where we stayed at Hotel Jolly, a fitting conclusion to a jolly event!

If you've been kind enough to read this far, you may have noticed I haven't written about my night terrors since my account of 1983. They had nevertheless been continuing. Over the years since then, the intensity was certainly diminishing, and the frequency also. It was my dearest wish, however, that I could get rid of them altogether. As I said, I would wake literally screaming in pure terror, with images of big black dogs attacking me. I would often be so shaking with fear that I would be afraid to go back to sleep.

I'm clear that various events have helped their decline. The year in London when I fully "found myself". Sadly, the death of my mother. Meeting Michael and 35 years of our life together. The Civil Partnership. Later, our marriage and our becoming Quakers and all that that led to which I will talk about in a later chapter. Writing this book has also been cathartic, as you can imagine. As I put this together in 2020, they have ALMOST completely disappeared. I believe now they will, at last, finally end. Nevertheless, it is an indication of the degree of trauma I was under when you consider it has taken literally decades to be free of them.

2007 was the year we toured Swing 'n' Sinatra, a big band style show with talented instrumentalists and vocalists. Our dates for that one took in the next year as well. Chris Smith and his band featured, along with his wife Simone who'd originally worked with the legendary Ivy Benson. Isn't it amazing how tastes vary? When talking to theatre managers about taking the show from us, most were keen. However, I clearly remember the manager at a provincial theatre saying to me "Anything to do with Sinatra is a complete no-no".

We also continued with our children's theatre tours.

Once again, Michael was the one with the idea. He is keen on poetry in general, and he suggested a show based on Edward Lear's "Owl and the Pussycat". We wrote the script together, Danny La Rue's musical director David Carter recorded all the backing tracks for the songs and dance routines, and Michael himself directed it. As usual, we auditioned and then rehearsed at a theatre in west London which was both on the tube and near to the M4.

It was a good show with good sets, good costumes and a good cast. However, the business wasn't so good. Things were well and truly fading now as regards ticket sales. The children's show market had moved to tv names in the main, and the most popular character was Peppa Pig. Ask a little girl if she'd rather see the Owl and the Pussycat or Peppa Pig and guess what the answer would be.

23 theatres took The Owl and the Pussycat including the Princess Theatre Hunstanton, Exmouth Pavilion, the Princess Royal Theatre Port Talbot, and the Concert Hall in Guernsey and, despite the reservations I've just expressed, the local paper's review re our performance at the Civic Theatre, Doncaster said "Just four actors, but what a show! A real treat for adults and children alike."

For our 2007 pantomime season, we presented Aladdin. It was a show we were really pleased with. We had a magnificent set which we'd bought from Richard Gill along with spectacular costumes, and Michael wrote a wonderful script. As it turned out, we only did Aladdin that one year. It was a great run, however, the show being taken by 28 theatres in all, including The Courtyard Theatre on the edge of Belfast where we did our usual 26 performances there, every one of them "house full". Aladdin included a terrific ultra-violet sequence in the cave with big illuminated figures dancing against a pitch black background. We put something similar into several of our pantomimes, using costumes, puppets and lighting we bought from a specialist ultra-violet company near Birmingham.

This is from the Exmouth Pavilion in Devon re our Aladdin pantomime.

"May I congratulate you on the success of your show. Thank you for coming to the Pavilion. Yet again, the feedback has been fantastic."

<u>2008</u>

Yet another terminal, Terminal 5, was opened at Heathrow. However, there were so many problems on the first day, that 500 flights had to be cancelled.

There was a worldwide financial crisis, a crash so severe that it resulted in the deepest recession we've ever known. Until now, that is. As I write in 2020 we have the coronavirus pandemic, which is proving to be even more devastating. We are currently in our second period of "lockdown" with more or less everything closed, and millions facing severe financial hardship.

Boris Johnson became Mayor of London, gaining fame for his Boris Bikes among other things!

Avid readers will recall Michael and myself meeting international superstar Anthony Newley backstage in his dressing room after one of his late-night cabarets at the Café Royal. He sadly passed away in 1999.

I remember him saying to us the best advice he was given when he started out in the business. On stage, be yourself writ large. Which is exactly what he used to do. In 2008, we toured a stylish and sophisticated tribute show The Anthony Newley Story, featuring vocalist Garth Bardsley and accompanists. Garth had written the authorised biography of Newley, "Stop the World, I Want to Get Off!" and had also recorded a CD album of Newley's most famous songs. It was a terrific show, one we were really proud of. We opened at Taunton Brewhouse Theatre and went all over the country, including a visit to the Broadway Theatre at Lewisham which Anthony Newley had himself played back in the early nineties when he first came back from the States after many years starring at Las Vegas. Michael and I had seen that performance, as had many in our audience in the same theatre fifteen years earler. Everyone was very complimentary about our show, and in particular, our star Garth Bardsley.

As a complete contrast, we also toured an Abba tribute show. I really can't bear the music of Abba, but we thought it would be a money-spinner. The troupe we chose, Abba Arrival, were very talented and very capable and it did good business for us at 11 theatres including venues as far apart as Luton, Stirling and Henley on Thames!

2008 also saw the last of our Bachelors Shows which we presented in a short season on Blackpool North Pier. The season also included the last of our Vince Hill shows which we presented at the same venue. With this being a seaside season, we featured the largest supporting cast we'd ever had. We had a proper finale walk-down and of course their act every night ended with a rendition of the No1 hit "I Believe". I would stand in the foyer as the audience walked out and every single night I heard people saying "Now that's what I call a show!" Have I mentioned that before?

Here's the review from the Blackpool Gazette.

"The boys performed and delivered a great show. Their timing, harmonies, professionalism, and sheer charisma of years in the business showed. An audience left the theatre last night in contentment of seeing stars that still leave many modern 'names' standing. By the way, I am only 48!"

Also that year, we created a brand new production of Robert Louis Stevenson's Treasure Island. Michael wrote the script in pantomime style and we again used the wonderful sets and designs of Richard Gill and Elizabeth Waghorn. We played 32 theatres with it, including 10 days at Lichfield Garrick, 5 days at Cwmbran Congress Theatre and visits to Hunstanton Princess, Bridlington Spa and many others.

We had these emails from audience members in different parts of the country. First, Matthew Jackson."I would just like to congratulate all the cast and crew of Treasure Island. It was absolutely fantastic. All the children in the audience were glued to the stage", and from Jenny Alves, "I have just taken my grandchildren to the Garrick Theatre to see Treasure Island. They loved it, a brilliant show that kept children and adults alike entertained."

2009

Woolworths announced the closure of all their 807 stores – a sign of what was to come for Britain's high streets.

Jazz musician Humphrey Littleton died, and playwright Harold Pinter. I remember trying to make head or tail of "The Caretaker" back in the 60s. In more recent years, we've enjoyed two or three different productions of this play, along with "The Birthday Party" and others of his. A bit of an acquired taste, I suppose.

The best production of "The Birthday Party" we've seen so far was at the National Theatre with Dora Bryan as the landlady. It was memorable for her outstanding performance, and also the great lighting which saw her semi-silhouetted through the serving hatch as she spoke to her guests from the kitchen. I'd met Dora at her flat in Brighton. Her agent had approached us re us taking over her one-woman show "Hello Dora!". She'd had a few problems and seemed to have heard through the grapevine that we'd be good to work with. Mainly. Her concerns were financial, around the profit venues were making from her performances, and the level of commission her agent was taking.

10% commission? 15%? Agent Eric Hall wasn't Dora's, but he was always renowned for taking a particularly healthy slice for himself. When asked if it was true that he took 20% of his clients' earnings, he replied "No. They take 80% of mine!"

But I digress. I got on with Dora very well and we had a few laughs together. However, with me not being given at all to patience, I rather "blew it" as they say nowadays.

She said she was having difficulties with her monologue "Daphne", and it wasn't going over well with audiences. It was a piece I knew well, written for her by Alan Melville back at the end of the fifties. We'd seen her do it at Chichester not long before and I had seen what I thought the problem was then. Being Mr Know-it-all, I immediately launched into a resume of my thoughts. If only I'd waited until she'd signed with us, I think she and I could have enjoyed working on it together and improved it no end. Anyway, I could soon tell that I'd said too much (not for the first time in my life!) and she was already daunted by the prospect of working with me. The meeting ended with her inviting us to visit any time we were in Brighton, just socially, and soon afterwards a letter came saying that she'd decided to stay with her current producer.

At this point I should say that I won't be able to write about all the different shows and tours that we did. It all becomes a blur! However, I must mention in passing the fabulous Beverley Sisters who worked for us. They were the original girl group, long before the Spice Girls, Little Mix, etc. Their act featured standards and comedy songs, and of course ended with their theme song and big hit "Sisters" by Irving Berlin.

Theatre Managers would write in the post to us after we'd appeared at their venue. We received this after our production of Little Red Riding Hood at Alton Assembly Rooms in Hampshire. "The show was an absolute delight with a great script, actors, costumes, songs and comedy, having a pace that kept both the young and the young at heart engaged for the whole performance. It was wonderful to see the whole audience having such a good time. I can honestly say that I have never seen a reaction to a show like yours at our venue."

And we had this from the Yvonne Arnaud Theatre, Guidford re our "Kate Adie's Inside Stories", in which we featured Kate relating her memories and anecdotes, interviewed by our good friend BBC Radio's Paul Harris, "We were thrilled by the response and feedback from the show."

Craig Wraight saw our Little Red Riding Hood show and sent this email. "My family and I watched your production of Red Riding Hood at the Bridlington Spa Theatre. Can I thank your cast for a wonderful show and making it a very enjoyable afternoon?"

We'd now re-cast our Joyce Grenfell show which had still been going on all this time. Maria Gibbs had moved abroad to New Zealand and we'd engaged Caroline Fields from BBC Radio's Friday Night is Music Night to take over as Joyce.

By 2009, Caroline had played the role 38 times in addition to the 82 shows Maria had done, and this year we wound things up with a final Joyce show at The Stables, Milton Keynes. This was a theatre owned by Cleo Laine and Johnny Dankworth and they lived next door. They came in to see the show, were most complimentary about Caroline's performance, and we have a picture of the three of them together after the show. It's on the wall in our flat here in Ferndown.

When we were in Yorkshire with this particular version of our Joyce show, the famous school inspector Gervase Phinn, a veteran of so many performances himself, was kind enough to write in The Yorkshire Post, "On a visit to Doncaster Civic Theatre, my wife and I lost ourselves in a wonderfully nostalgic evening filled with the gentle humour we so much enjoy. Caroline Fields delighted her audience with sketches and songs written and once performed by the inimitable Joyce Grenfell."

Spring 2009 saw the last tour of our New Adventures of Pinocchio. By the time we'd finished that particular outing with it, we'd played 170 theatres in all with the various versions of Pinocchio we'd created. What a run.

In the summer, I was at a big gay party at a big house in Earls Court. There was a swimming pool in the garden and during the afternoon numerous handsome young men in the skimpiest of trunks were jumping in and out of the water in the bright sunshine.

I have never been able to sit in the sun, and so I found myself a spot in the shade under a tree. This turned out to be another of those pivotal events that happen in life.

Definitely another "meant to be!"

There was only one other person sitting there and we got talking. He was maybe ten years older than me and his name was Barry Brown. He said that he didn't like direct sunlight either. We chatted away and he discovered that I was a theatre producer and I discovered that he was a television producer, having produced a number of successful series for the BBC including Barry Norman's Film Night. I was very interested in his stories of meeting and working with various stars, and he was very interested in my account of our Joyce Grenfell tours and others. Mary Tyler Moore had proved to be the most difficult of the Hollywood actresses he'd worked with, he said, bringing with her a whole entourage to communicate her demands to him.

To cut a long story short, Barry and I talked most of the afternoon and quickly struck up a friendship that was to last until his death from Parkinson's Disease ten years later. Barry had been working on cruise ships, telling all his stories of film stars and backstage life at the BBC. He said he'd been accompanied on the most recent cruise by a very talented actor called Gerald Dickens who was actually the great great grandson of the legendary author. Gerald performed a kind of "best of Dickens" one man show, which had been going down very well on board ship and he'd been saying to Barry that he'd love to be able to perform his one-man shows in small theatres, but just didn't know how to go about it.

Barry put Gerald in touch with me, we met up and did a deal, and Michael and I went on to present Gerald at over 150 theatres altogether all over the UK, right until we retired at the end of 2017. In fact, the very last professional show that we presented was Gerald Dickens in A Christmas Carol. The final performances were at Leicester Guildhall, a favourite venue of ours, and we had two full houses for both the matinee and the evening shows.

2009 was the year we went on our own first cruise. We sailed from Tilbury to Norway on the Marco Polo, a traditional-style adults-only ship, saw the magnificent fjords, and visited Bergen where we paid the equivalent of £10 for two small cups of black coffee.

We enjoyed the experience on ship, and have since been on three more cruises, including a round Britain one which sailed as far north as the Orkneys where we visited Kirkwall Cathedral. We stopped also at Tobermory, Dublin, and the Scilly Isles amongst other places, before completing the circle and arriving back at Tilbury.

We've also tried Saga Cruises, and have been hugely impressed. Sailing from Southampton is much more convenient than Tilbury, particularly when they send a private car to our door to take us to the port. Everything on board is really wonderful including the catering, the cabins, and the entertainment.

Also that year, I met Simon Cole. He has become a good friend of ours and has been tremendously helpful in running our websites and, more recently, converting all our scripts, etc. into Kindle ebooks and paperbacks which are now available on Amazon.

In 2009, we decided to put together a production of the first pantomime I'd ever seen in Southampton all those years earlier, Mother Goose. It was a good show and we were really pleased with it on a number of levels, including audience reaction. Michael wrote a wonderful script and once again directed the whole production, we had a good strong cast, and a nice new set which Simon helped to create. We'd inherited a charming Priscilla the Goose costume when we bought out the touring children's theatre company in 2000, but had never so far used it. We were booked once again for 26 performances at the Courtyard

Theatre, Belfast and then we took the whole show on to Wrexham, Morecambe, Abergavenny and Skipton over the Christmas period. However, for a number of reasons, we decided that would be our last pantomime season.

<u>2010</u>

Gordon Brown ended his premiership with a general election which resulted in a hung parliament, and a coalition government between the Conservatives and Lib Dems. David Cameron was Prime Minister and Nick Clegg was Deputy. Seeing the two of them in their smart suits together in the garden at Number 10, many in the media likened them to a same-sex couple at the now increasingly common civil partnerships!

The new parliament also contained Britain's first Green MP in the shape of Caroline Lucas, and on that note, it was recorded that in 2010 badgers started to breed again in Scotland for the first time in 400 years.

Jazz musician Johnny Dankworth died. As I said in my entry for last year, he and his wife Cleo Laine had owned and run a 400 seat theatre next to their home in Milton Keynes. It mainly hosted jazz events, but we did play it a few times including the Joyce Grenfell event I wrote about, and we had a full house there for one of our Dickens shows.

Other deaths that year included the fine Scottish singer Kenneth McKellar, one of my favourites. Who remembers the days when the BBC used to have a Hogmanay show on New Years Eve? It was in 2010 that we met the charming

Scottish singer Moira Anderson at a showbiz party. I suggested to her she might like to do one of our "evening with" shows, with just her and a pianist, but she sadly replied "I don't think many people would want to spend an evening with me". Was she right? We shall never know!

Another passing that year was talented ventriloquist Ray Alan. Remember him with his dummy "Lord Charles"? He was just about the best "vent" we ever had. You could NEVER see his lips move at all, even for "bottle of beer".

Strangely, one time when we were at the Grand Theatre Wolverhampton, we stayed at the Britannia Hotel next door. When we came down to breakfast, we discovered Ray and his wife in the dining room. We hadn't realised they were staying there as well. They invited us to share a table with them and we had a very pleasant chat. When we all got up to go, I was reminded just how tall he was. I'm only 5'7" now. I seem to get shorter every year. I was once 5'9". Then 5'8". Ask me again in a few years' time.

Anyway, he must have been 6'3" or 4", and just towered above me as he shook my hand. The first line in his stage act was always "Taller than you thought, isn't he?" - going by the fact that his audience had probably only ever seen him on tv. He was another of the last real variety acts. He relied on talent and charm, two attributes commonly missing nowadays. He didn't see the need to swear every few seconds, or treat us to his own particular political views.

This was the year of our final outing with Titter Ye Not! This time, in liaison with Paul Harris, we called it Frankie Titters On! Paul did nine more shows for us, opening at the Palace Theatre Newark and then going everywhere from Oldham Coliseum to the Ashcroft at Croydon. Michael was Company Stage Manager, very capably as always. Something I really couldn't begin to do!

Here's the review from Viewpoint Magazine when we played "Titter" near to home at the Barrington Theatre, Ferndown.

"Paul Harris brought Howerd to life with a passion, and the jokes and catchphrases rumbled out with the audience enjoying every minute."

While I'm mentioning reviews, I should also mention Dame Diana Rigg, who has recently passed away. We'd seen her great performance in Stephen Sondheim's "Follies" in the West End, which no doubt garnered her wonderful reviews. Diana always enjoyed the really questionable reviews that some of her fellow performers received. Here's a review of John Osborn's radical, new-age play "Look Back in Anger" that she quotes in her humorous book "No Turn Unstoned".

"The dramatist of Look Back in Anger we are told, feels that as a representative of the younger generation he has every right to be angry. Some of his audience may be angrier still, but not for the same reason."

And Denis Quilley as Charles Condomine in Noel Coward's Blithe Spirit got the following notice when he opened his morning's paper.

"Denis Quilley played the role with all the charm and animation of the leg of a billiard table."

Of course, 2010 was the year of my 60th birthday. We had a big party at Wimborne's Allendale Centre, and so many people were there. We had music from Three Monarchs star David Conway on the harmonica, and we had the most amazing close-up magic from a professional magician, Richard Campbell, working his way around all the tables. My dear friend Edith came all the way from Skipton, and stayed over at the Kings Head, just to be with us. I have a lovely photo of her with my teaching colleague Trish and my college friend Alun, two other guests at the party. It was the last picture of Edith as she passed away soon afterwards.

Also, for my 60th birthday, my dear friend tv producer Barry Brown took me to lunch in London, as he wasn't able to get away to Dorset on the day of the party. He chose Launceston Place, which he told me had been Diana Princess of Wales' favourite restaurant. You could see why. Hidden away, not far from Goodge St, you would never find it unless you knew, which I certainly didn't! We had a wonderful meal, just the two of us, in a very quiet setting, which is just how I like it.

2011

VAT was increased from 17.5% to 20% and sixty HMV stores closed.

There was much celebration throughout the nation when Prince William married Catherine Middleton in Westminster Abbey. Teachers went on strike over pensions.

The UK population increased by almost half a million in one year, the biggest increase since 1961, and there were violent riots in London, Birmingham, Liverpool, Nottingham, and Bristol.

50% of the population now owned a mobile phone.

Beatle Paul McCartney married American heiress Nancy Shevell, and actress Elizabeth Taylor died, together with boxer Henry Cooper and screenwriter David Croft. Croft was a local man, born in Sandbanks, and had given us some of our best and most enduring comedies. Dad's Army, Are You Being Served?, It Ain't Half Hot Mum, Hi De Hi, You Rang M'Lord, and Oh Doctor Beeching! were all his. What a talent, and what a legacy.

2011 also saw the death of "Sir" Jimmy Savile, an event which proved quite pivotal in a number of ways.

Out of the blue, we were contacted by the agency representing opera singer Lesley Garrett. An agent by the name of Louise Badger was looking after Lesley and she wanted to know if we'd be interested in presenting a theatre tour of An Evening with Lesley Garrett - Britain's Favourite Soprano. I went to meet Louise at the Hilton Hotel at

Newbury and with just the one meeting, she and I made a deal. Lesley would sing some of her favourite songs with piano accompaniment, relate lots of her behind-the-scenes stories, and answer questions from the audience. We engaged our good friend Paul Harris to interview Lesley each night on stage and field the questions to her.

What a wonderful talent Lesley turned out to be, and what a lovely lady. She invited us to her Hampstead home, and introduced us to her GP husband.

Lesley did two tours for us. We opened the first in 2011 at Harpenden Public Halls and then took in theatres across the country from the Ashcroft at Croydon to Buxton Opera House. Well it was opera!

I think the third date on the tour was when I realised something strange. I was selling the programmes in the foyer as usual and recognised a man buying one. I said "Didn't I sell you a programme yesterday?" He agreed that was the case. Here we were in North Wales, and the day before we'd been in Croydon. He'd been there at both theatres. "Well", I said, "This will only be the same as I sold you then. All the programmes are the same. There's nothing different in today's".

"Yes I know", he said," but I'll have one all the same".

The we noticed that everywhere we went, the same man was there, whether it was the north or the south, the west country, East Anglia or Wales, he was always there and he

217

always bought a programme. He sat every time in the middle of the front row.

I mentioned this to Lesley. She wasn't in the least surprised. She said one time she'd appeared in Australia at the Sydney Opera House. She walked out on the stage and he was there, sitting in the middle of the front row!

As a measure of what a lovely lady Lesley is, one day she told us it was this particular fan's 60th birthday. He'd written to her to say so. She'd bought him a birthday cake and wanted to invite him into her dressing room to cut the cake and blow out the candle. Would we go and sit in with her as chaperones? She just wanted to be careful.

Very wise, but such a very thoughtful gesture towards a loyal fan. It made one man's day – or maybe year!

We were very pleased when the following year Lesley toured for us again, and this time we visited the Floral Pavilion at New Brighton, Harrogate Theatre, and South Shields Customs House amongst many others. We were even booked locally by our Tivoli Theatre in Wimborne where several of our loyal friends came along to the full house.

We had two very happy tours with Lesley, but it was time for us all to move on. When she left us after the last show, she made a very wise comment. I think Michael and I must have already been giving the impression that we were going to have to start winding down and she said, "It eats you up and spits you out. That's showbusiness." Very true.

Julie Andrews once remarked that while you may love showbusiness, showbusiness will never love you back. Unless you've worked in the profession, you may find this hard to fathom. If you have, you will understand.

Rupert Everett has commented, "There's not much point telling the truth in showbusiness because nobody listens."

It is undoubtedly just about the most insecure profession there is, totally hand-to-mouth, but we all seem to love it – or why would we stay?

Enthused by our excursion into light opera, we decided to follow up with another tour in the same vein. We engaged young opera star Jonathan Ansell who'd won tv talent show The X Factor with his group G4. Jonathan had gone solo, and was ideal for the "evening with" format we were now using. I interviewed Jonathan on stage each night leading into the various songs he performed with keyboard accompaniment. We went everywhere from Hartlepool to Felixstowe with Jonathan and, like we found with Lesley Garrett, we soon realised that we were being followed everywhere we went. A group of slightly older women were always at the Stage Door and some of them could be very demanding!

We departed from our usual showbiz style with the first of our football shows. Once again, Paul Harris agreed to be the host and interviewer, and we called the evening "Tommy Docherty on the Ball". Five theatres booked it, including the Kings at Southsea and the Palace Theatre, Newark. We were amazed at the detailed knowledge of the fans in the questions they asked when we threw it open to the audience. Paul fielded the questions and Tommy provided the answers.

Here's the review from the local paper after our appearance at Colne Municipal Hall in Lancashire.

"We were fortunate to spend a couple of hours in the company of one of the great living legends of football. Tommy Docherty is a fantastic speaker with a wealth of football knowledge and lots of funny stories."

Not long after, we followed up with another similar presentation, this time featuring Lawrie McMenemy who, once again, was On the Ball as far as we were concerned. We played Bournemouth Pavilion with Lawrie among other venues.

We'd told Lawrie about our good friends Gary and Mo Tomlinson who do a lot of charity work, and he turned up with several souvenir colour photos which he'd signed for them to sell.

2012

The Queen celebrated her Diamond Jubilee after 60 years on the throne, and Britain hosted the 2012 Olympic Games.

An inquiry was launched into the sexual behaviour of BBC presenter Jimmy Savile.

Scientists reported a 25% decline in UK birdlife.

Comedian Frank Carson died. We'd been with him one night at a theatre somewhere when someone asked him why he wasn't on the television any more. He replied, "Homosexuals. That's why. All the tv is run by bloody homosexuals now."

Legendary guitarist Bert Weedon died. As I've said, he worked for us just once, during our summer season at Clacton in 2004, and we thought he was the most lovely man. A perfect gentleman. Do you remember him on Five O'Clock Club with Wally Whyton and Muriel Young?

Bee Gee Robin Gibb also died, along with Eric Sykes and Clive Dunn ("Permission to speak Sir?") Actress Daphne Oxenford passed away at the age of 93. How many of us can still recall her on Listen with Mother each afternoon asking "Are you sitting comfortably? Then I'll begin."?

We also lost Max Bygraves. We'd met him a few times at events, but he never worked for us. Not everyone's favourite, his critics couldn't see how perfectly polished his act always was. People in the business would marvel at how he was utterly relaxed on stage, completely confident that he could hold the audience in the palm of his hand singlehandedly for an hour or more - which he always did. To his fans, his shows were like a big party to which you'd been invited as friends.

"I was one of a big family. We used to have octopus for Christmas dinner. It didn't taste very good, but a least everyone got a leg."

He was a very astute businessman. Not everyone knows that in 1959 he bought the rights to the musical "Oliver" from Lionel Bart who was going through hard times. Max paid Lionel £350, and then sold the musical a decade later for a quarter of a million. Max wrote many of his own songs including "You Need Hands".

Since his father died, we've met up a few times with Anthony Bygraves who still lives in Bournemouth.

It was in 2012 that we engaged Lonnie Donegan's son Peter to tour The Lonnie Donegan Story for us. We included all of Lonnie's hits from Rock Island Line to My Old Man's a Dustman, and I interviewed Peter on stage in a few segments between the songs. This particular tour opened at the Palace Theatre, Paignton.

Another new departure for us in 2012 was our antiques show with Jonty Hearnden from tv's Cash in the Attic. We did a very enjoyable tour with him. I interviewed Jonty on stage each night, and fielded the audience questions. He brough along several of his own interesting items each time, and the public were invited to bring artefacts for Jonty to discuss and value during the show.

We were at the theatre in Abertillery one night when a lady turned up with a pretty ordinary looking plate. Her face was a picture when Jonty told her it was worth at least £1000!

Spurred on by the success of our "evening withs" (and with the ease of presenting them!), we put our heads together to think of some other good candidates for this treatment. We decided to approach the agent of cricket umpire legend Dickie Bird, who seemed to be such a popular figure, well-spoken of wherever he was mentioned.

After a chat with Patsy, his agent, I drove up to Barnsley to meet Dickie at his little cottage on the edge of the town. He proudly showed me his big red "This is your Life" book, and all the pictures on the walls of him with everyone from Princess Margaret to Margaret Thatcher. I took some photos of Dickie in his back garden which we then used on the posters for the tour. Once again, we engaged Paul Harris to interview Dickie on stage. Dickie was mobbed after every performance with a long queue of punters wanting to speak to him in the foyer. We took Dickie from Blackpool Grand to the Northampton Royal, and many more in between. The most amazing thing about the tour was Paul Harris. Paul knew absolutely nothing about cricket, and didn't have the slightest interest in it, but you would never have guessed, watching him on stage. His well-rehearsed banter with Dickie was completely convincing every time!

Stage Eight: Winding Down.

In which we present our final children's theatre tour, and start to find new priorities.

<u>2013</u>

Margaret Thatcher died at the age of 87. Street parties were held in several towns and cities to "celebrate" her death, and a week later the Wizard of Oz song "Ding Dong the Witch is Dead" entered the singles chart at number ten.

The funeral for Baroness Thatcher, as she then had become, was held at St Paul's Cathedral where, equally, many others mourned. She'd been Britain's first female Prime Minister. For some, she was the wrong kind of woman. For others, she'd saved us from disaster. Very much the Marmite Premier.

The largest public library ever built in Britain opened in Birmingham, and part of the ceiling of the Apollo Theatre in the West End fell down, injuring 81 people.

Computer pioneer and WWII codebreaker Alan Turing, who had done so much for the nation and had been chemically castrated following his conviction and public shaming for his homosexuality, was given a posthumous royal pardon.

Once again, the list of notable deaths gets longer. It included this year jazz musicians Kenny Ball and Terry Lightfoot, along with actor Richard Briers ("The Good Life").

Noel Harrison, son of Rex, who had one rather memorable hit with "Windmills of Your Mind", passed away, and we lost Mike Winters, half of much-loved double act Mike and Bernie Winters.

Mike and Bernie were just about the only British variety artistes of note that I never saw on stage, and I do regret that. I thought their act was charming, funny and polished. Disc jockey David Jacobs passed away ("Hello there!") along with Sir David Frost. We'd only just met Sir David a few months previously. He came to Lichfield Garrick Theatre where we were seasoned regulars and the manager Adrian gave us a couple of house seats. Get-in time was always three hours before performance time, to allow for any mishaps, traffic delays, etc. Half an hour before curtain up, there was still no sign of Sir David. I said to one of the stage hands "Are you looking out for his car?" and he replied "No! Knowing him, we're waiting for his helicopter!" Anyway, the great man made it just in time. "Hello, good evening, and welcome!"

He treated the audience to all his stories of everyone from President Nixon to Princess Diana. He was, as were so many in those days, most charming to talk to and a perfect gentleman. Informed readers will know that Sir David's father was a Methodist minister. I always admired David Frost. One of the things he used to say was that you could learn SOMETHING from absolutely everyone you meet. Very true, and a good attitude to have.

Two of the artistes who'd worked for us very successfully also went to the big theatre in the sky – Stan Stennett and Joan Regan.

On a different note, I was fitted with dentures! Never blessed with particularly good teeth, I'd sat in a succession of dentists' chairs too many times to count over the years. Now the row of crowns that had been fitted top front had given way. It was only a bread roll, but I felt the whole row snap off as I bit into it.

The dentist said, "It's always a bread roll".

Anyway, to cut a long story short, I now have partial dentures built on a thin metal plate which sits in my mouth during the day, and in a bowl in the bathroom overnight. Generally, I'm very pleased with them, but definitely a sign of old age approaching. What would Pam Ayres say?

(Answer, for those not sure, "I wish I'd looked after me teeth!")

I should mention that, without the dentures and with only one tooth remaining centre, top, front, I look like a cross between Bugs Bunny and the Wicked Witch of the West. Not a pretty sight!

Locally, I came across a talented man by the name of Clive St James who was performing a Tommy Cooper tribute show. Clive was very funny, just like Tommy himself, and he had the great man off to a tee. To cut a long story short, we toured "The Best of Tommy Cooper – Just Like That" to theatres all over the UK, even going over to Belfast and up to the Georgian Theatre Royal in Yorkshire. Once again, Michael was the ever willing, never complaining Company stage Manager.

We were really getting into our new style of celebrity "evening with ..." shows and I had the idea of a gardening show where people could come along and ask questions about their shrubs or their strawberries. We approached the agency representing Charlie Dimmock who was pleased to do these for us.

 Charlie lives at Romsey, not far away, and she and I met up to plan everything. I would interview her on stage in the first half, when we would go through a well-rehearsed selection of her anecdotes about her time with Alan Titchmarsh on Ground Force on tv. Then in the second half, I'd throw it open for the audience to share their gardening questions. Michael would tour the stalls with a roving mike, and Charlie and I would respond. We went to theatres everywhere and Charlie was warmly received. We were completely bowled over by her knowledge of everything horticultural. Quite amazing. It was a very happy tour of 12 theatres from Epsom Playhouse to Theatr Brycheiniog at Brecon, and we ended up in Runcorn if I remember rightly.

2013 was nothing if not varied. We also took out a little wartime show which we called Hits from the Blitz. There seemed to be quite an interest in that kind of thing at the time, and it was a good little show which did reasonable business at 8 theatres from Gorleston Pavilion to Bury St Edmunds Theatre Royal.

2013 was the year we finally brought the curtain down on our children's shows. Our Little Red Riding hood tour had been soldiering on, with Michael directing the actors, driving the van, liaising with each theatre's technicians, and generally managing the tour. I booked all the hotels, and turned up once in a while myself.

Business was not what it was, however. When we first bought that big children's theatre production company from Steve and Patrick 13 years earlier, every venue would typically book two performances, both of which were frequently sold out. Over the years this had gradually become one show at each venue, and then the venues were becoming smaller. Instead of Bournemouth Pavilion it would be Wimborne Tivoli. Instead of Blackpool Grand it would be Darwen Library Theatre.

We decided to call it a day, and just concentrate on our celebrity shows and our Charles Dickens shows with Gerald Dickens. All these were so easy to stage. No choreographer, no scenery, no weeks of rehearsals, etc. etc.

Our final Red Riding Hood show was at the Ashcroft Theatre Croydon, and it coincided with Michael's 50th birthday.

We had a big after-show party and invited all the cast. Many of our friends and family travelled long distances to be with us. Our friends Karen and David came from Bude in

Cornwall and thereby won the prize for having made the longest journey to be there – a souvenir poster signed by Red Riding Hood herself!

Cousins John and Wendy came from Wimborne, and my good friend tv producer Barry Brown managed to get himself there, even though his Parkinson's was much more advanced by then. Shirley and Sandy joined us, Shirley having worked so tirelessly as our Administrator in our early days as impresarios. It was lovely that Michael's sister Shelagh, now my sister-in-law, came, along with our nephew Max.

A wonderful event, and a fitting end to 13 years of nationwide children's theatre tours.

<u>2014</u>

Once again, there were extensive floods across the UK. This has become a regular occurrence in recent years, and can only be due to global warming.

An Oxfordshire councillor blamed the floods on the government's decision to allow gay weddings, which had apparently angered God.

Part of the railway at Dawlish on the south coast of Devon was washed away, severing the only remaining line into Cornwall and cutting the county off completely from the rail network. Following the Conservative government's closure of numerous Devon and Cornwall branch lines after the

Beeching Report in the sixties, sadly the Labour government that followed didn't do any better.

In 1968 they closed the alternative inland main line to Cornwall via Okehampton and Tavistock, leaving only the coastal route which runs within a few yards of the sea. All trains have to go this way now, and whenever the sea breaches it, which happens with increasing regularity, every service is suspended and "buses replace trains", sometimes for weeks on end.

The first same-sex weddings were held in March, and we ourselves converted our civil partnership into a marriage a few months later. We went back to Ferndown Registry Office and paid £4 to Dorset County Council. It was just us and the Registrar this time. No friends, no family, no witnesses even. He took our four pounds, tapped out a few things on his computer and then stood up to shake our hands as he announced that we'd now been married since the date of the civil partnership 7 years earlier. He was very pleasant, judging the whole thing just right. As we got up to leave he said "Now which of you two gentlemen is going to carry the other over the threshold?"

We decided to go on another honeymoon (our third) and set off once again for Brussels by Eurostar.

Tony Blair and David Cameron, on opposite sides of the political spectrum, both come to mind.

When Tony Blair left office, he said he thought introducing civil partnerships had brought more joy than anything else he'd done.

When David Cameron left office, he said the thing he was most proud of was introducing same-sex marriage.

The C of E voted to allow women to become Bishops, and Scots voted "no" to independence. Nicola Sturgeon succeeded Alex Salmond as leader of the Scottish Nationalists.

Tony Benn died at the age of 88, along with Dora Bryan (91), and Donald Sinden (90). "Stranger on the Shore" clarinettist Acker Bilk also passed away. Everyone knows his hit record, but who remembers the 1961 drama series of the same title, of which it was the haunting theme? All I can say is I think it was on Saturdays at teatime, and was about an immigrant. That's all I can remember, although I think I quite enjoyed it at the time.

Back in 1986, when we first met, Michael had just started going to Bournemouth Quakers at their Meeting House in Boscombe. I've already described how we tried this together, along with other denominations, but quickly found it was impossible to go to the other churches without being quizzed as to who exactly we were. Were we brothers? Why were we together? Had we left our wives at home?

Now, in 2014, Michael wanted to try Quakers again. I was an Anglican through and through, but hadn't been able to attend for many years for the reasons already stated. At

Bournemouth this time, I quite quickly found the style of silent worship appealing. We soon came to the conclusion that it would be good to be based in Quakers, but go out from there to other events more widely. A perfect complement to the Quaker stillness and contemplation is the William Temple Association with its programme of interesting after-dinner speakers. I'd so enjoyed their meetings back in the 70s, so we decided to pursue both. An ideal combination.

We ended 2014 with a short run of Charles Dickens' A Christmas Carol. Gerald Dickens did his own tour of this one every year in America during December, and this meant that we could only do a handful of these in the UK once he was back. Theatres would only take it before Christmas, never after. This particular year we played to a full house at Wavendon Stables Theatre, another full house at Gloucester Guildhall, and a further full house (twice) at Leicester Guildhall. We invited my college friend Revd Roger Wheelhouse and his wife Sue to the Gloucester show and they loved it. I think they really enjoyed going backstage afterwards for a private chat with the star!

<u>2015</u>

Although we were welcomed at Bournemouth Quakers, we were finding it difficult to become part of a group which was 12 miles away from us in Boscombe.

Just at this time, a new Meeting was launched in Wimborne and we went there on week three. Soon we had found our niche.

After a while, Michael became a Member, and I followed soon after, joining the list of showbusiness Quaker "Friends" who include Dame Judi Dench, the late David Jacobs, Sheila Hancock and Victoria Wood's magician husband Geoffrey Durham.

Michael and I both do voluntary work now through the Quakers and in the wider community. Who knew I could be a committee person? Wonders will never cease!

Chancellor George Osborne announced that tackling terrorism would be a priority after numerous incidents, including the murderous Charlie Hebdo attacks in Paris.

UK inflation rate fell to zero for the first time in history, and Tesco reported a record £6.4 billion loss.

Libby Lane became the first woman to be ordained Bishop by the Church of England. The Church of Scotland announced they would ordain openly gay men who were in civil partnerships.

At the General Election, the coalition ended with the Conservatives winning an outright majority. Lib Dems were almost wiped out, securing just 8 of their previous 57 seats, and former Lib Dem leader Charles Kennedy died of alcoholism at the age of 55. Tim Farron became leader, and Jeremy Corbin became leader of the Labour Party.

A ceremony at Runnymede marked the 800th anniversary of Magna Carter.

In two happier "green" moves, a 5p charge was introduced on plastic carrier bags, which resulted in an 80% decrease in their use, and part of the former Waverley Route railway was reopened in Scotland. This had been one of several important 100 mile-long main lines closed between 1968 and 1970. It had run from Carlisle to Edinburgh via Hawick and Melrose. The northern section between Edinburgh and Tweedbank was reopened by the Queen, and usage has been around 4 times what was predicted.

As I write in 2020, the government is considering 50 reopening schemes which would put back some of the devastation caused by the Conservative government's Beeching cuts and those of the following Labour administration under Harold Wilson and Barbara Castle. How far any of these new schemes will get now is anybody's guess, as rail usage has fallen by almost 90% due to the coronavirus pandemic.

Michael and I had seen the vacant and overgrown track bed north of Galashiels when we went on a coach holiday to Melrose in 2012. When we went in 2019 to stay in a self-catering cottage at St Boswells, we were able to travel on the line into Edinburgh, passing through the most beautiful countryside in swift comfort.

Much-loved singer and entertainer Cilla Black died. There was an outpouring of grief from the nation similar to that shown for Princess Diana. A "lorra lorra love."

Another loss that year was "Oliver" actor Ron Moody. (You got to pick a pocket or two.) A few years earlier, his agent had invited us to a charity event he was hosting at the New Theatre, Oxford and, much as I'd greatly enjoyed his performances as Fagin both on stage and on screen, I can't say I found him at all agreeable to talk to. We met him in his dressing room before the show, and perhaps it was just pre-show nerves. Anyway, afterwards, it was difficult to know what to say when his agent asked us what we'd thought of him!

Our close friend Peter Franklin died in Brighton. He had been hugely successful with his puppet collaboration with Stephen Lee, and their artistry and flair had given them acclaim. However, he'd been declining in health for a long time and finally passed away just before Christmas. This was a great loss to us. We'd enjoyed numerous theatre trips with Stephen and Peter to the West End, to Chichester and elsewhere, we'd had so many great meals out with them, with the conversations raising so many laughs. We'd even shared a table at the Water Rats Ball at Grosvenor House. Now he was gone and Stephen was left alone.

As a one-off, our good friend Gerald Dickens performed Charles Dickens' The Signalman for us at one of our favourite venues Leicester Guildhall, which linked back to the small local tour we'd done with that piece, performed by Raymond Sargent in Dorset a decade or more before.

Gerald's year-round Dickens tours were continuing, with Michael acting as Company Stage Manager everywhere, plotting and calling the lighting cues he'd created for the productions. We mainly did Gerald's one-man versions of Great Expectations, Nicholas Nickleby, and a sort of "best of" Audience with Charles Dickens. We took Gerald everywhere from Lancaster Grand to Blackfriars Arts Centre, Boston.

Some quirky venues included Theatr Harlech on the Cambrian Coast, and locally the Layard Theatre at Canford Magna just 4 miles from our home.

Other Dickens venues also included Camberley Theatre, which Michael and I had played ourselves about 15 years earlier with our World of Puppets, and we went three times with Gerald to the Princess Theatre, Burnham on Sea.

<u>2016</u>

There were more extensive floods, more stabbings, and in the midlands, even tornadoes! Client Earth won their case against the government over dangerous levels of air pollution in the UK.

A new national living wage was introduced for the first time, and Labour MP Jo Cox was stabbed to death in a far-right assassination attack. There was a twelve-hour riot at HMP Birmingham involving 600 inmates, and the longest rail strike in history.

The big event of the year (of the century?) was the Referendum, which resulted in Britain voting to leave the EU by a tiny margin. The vote was 52% to leave, and 48% to remain. Michael and I both voted to remain.

This brought about the beginning of several years of wrangling during which the nation became increasingly divided and fractured. I have voted for all three main parties in my time and I am not generally partisan, so I hope readers won't object to my stating which way we voted above.

Amongst our own circles, there are people who voted both ways, and I completely respect either opinion. I can't see why the vote should result in people falling out, but families and communities were ripped apart by the outcome of the Referendum. Wounds that are yet to heal.

The first fallout from the surprise Referendum result was Prime Minister David Cameron's resignation the following day. He was replaced by Theresa May.

This was the year we lost several legendary radio disc-jockeys. Ed Stewart whom we'd met at Connie Creighton's funeral and found most charming, Sir Terry Wogan, and Sir Jimmy Young. Keen readers will remember that Jimmy Young was Auntie Grace's favourite, and he was also a favourite of ours. When we were doing our schools tours in the mid nineties, we'd sit in our van at lunchtime listening to him on the radio while eating our daily rations. He was much more than a disc-jockey, being a capable, astute political interviewer and, in an earlier setting, a very pleasant singer. He was a "crooner", as they used to call them, along with people like Bing Crosby, and had several chart hits including two No 1s – "The Man from Laramie" and "Unchained Melody". One of our tour bookers, a freelance, was also engaged to book the theatre tour that Jimmy Young did after he'd been dropped by the BBC from his daily radio show. He gave us a couple of tickets to see Sir Jimmy at Poole Arts Centre but there was no singing, just an interview in which he related among other things his feelings about the BBC. Not a very satisfying evening.

Three more great entertainers passed away – Paul Daniels, Ronnie Corbett, and Victoria Wood. We'd met Paul a few times. Few know that, as well as being an extremely accomplished illusionist, he was also a very capable hypnotist. Our good friends Stephen and Peter had been on the Paul Daniels Christmas Show on BBC1 with their puppets one year.

Ronnie Corbett was a close friend of Danny La Rue and he was often at Danny's parties, but we didn't really get to know him. Do you remember his monologues, sitting in that oversized chair?

"Last week our young puppy accidentally swallowed the remote control for the tv. A bit unfortunate. Now we have to twiddle his tummy to get BBC1. If we want ITV, we have to twiddle the top of his leg. Thank God we never watch BBC2."

Stephanie Booth died. I'd met Stephanie and worked with her quite a bit when doing my voiceovers in the nineties. She was born Keith Hull, had been married and even fathered two children. She'd subsequently gone through gender reassignment and then surgery, and was now "married" to a man. She'd shared much of her story with me over the years, and I can't begin to tell you what she'd been through. Her parents were Jehovah's Witnesses.

Can you imagine their reaction when she told them about her change? She was completely disowned and shunned. A few years before she died, she'd attempted a reconciliation with them, as she was beside herself with grief over their treatment of her. On the appointed day, only one of them agreed to meet her in what was a "one-off", very strained event.

In recent years, she'd bought a chain of hotels in North Wales, including the Chainbridge at Berwyn near Llangollen, one of our favourite places. She invited me to lunch at her new hotel, where I met her husband David for the first time, and they served me Welsh Black Beef. You could sit in the lounge and watch the little steam trains pull up at the tiny Berwyn Station on the opposite side of the river. It was an idyllic spot.

I empathised with her enormously, and we got on well. She was a very astute businesswoman and had persuaded a television company to produce a reality series "Hotel Stephanie" which ran for two series and of course widely promoted her hotels. She told me that of all the many business people she'd had dealings with over the years, I was the only one she felt she could trust.

They'd also bought a farm at Corwen, just along the Dee valley, and she told me it was her "little piece of heaven". It was at her farm that she was tragically killed in a tractor accident. After all she'd been through, she was gone. I hope she is now at peace, and I believe she is. She gave me her autobiography, "Stephanie, a girl in a million" and it's still here on the shelf.

We finally decided it was time to bring the curtain down on most of our remaining shows. The travelling was becoming increasingly arduous and audience numbers were smaller. Theatres were less and less willing to pay guarantees for performances, expecting us to take the risk not only on the artiste fees and touring costs, but now also on the ticket sales. (See Appendix 6.)

We decided to cease everything else and just carry on with the Dickens shows a bit longer. Soon those would need to end as well.

Keen readers will remember that Michael's favourite singer is Bob Dylan, so what better way to end our music shows than with a "Best of Bob Dylan" show!

We remembered a wonderful, talented husband and wife duo called Andante who'd worked for us many times a few years before. They would be ideal. Their names are Vee Sweeney and Mark Rowson. Innovative, versatile, they could create some stunning arrangements of Dylan songs. We got in touch with them again, and went up to visit them at their home in Birmingham.

At the time, they were supporting Sir Ken Dodd in his nationwide theatre tour. They invited us to see them in Ken's show at the Princess Theatre, Torquay, a theatre we knew well. The show started at 7.30 and at about 8 o'clock, Andante did a twenty minute spot showcasing their slick multi-instrumental act. At 8.20 they were back in their dressing room, where they would have to remain until 1 o'clock in the morning when the show would finally end. Ken would say "How about a big round of applause for my special guest stars Andante!" They'd run on while the audience were clapping away, and join Ken waving as the curtain came down. Then, and only then, could they finally pack everything into their van and drive back to their hotel for a very well-earned rest!

We enjoyed their act, and the show overall, but weren't there to see the finale. We'd seen Ken at the London Palladium in the mid nineties, and on that occasion we'd left at the interval, which came about half past ten. Bernard Cribbins and his wife were next to us, and they were leaving as well, with Bernard saying he just couldn't take any more!

This time, we'd been invited to meet Ken in his dressing room AFTER the show! By that time, we were fast asleep in our hotel.

You don't always have to accept an invitation.

Perhaps you'll remember George Bernard Shaw receiving one in the post saying "Lady Proctor will be at home on Tuesday afternoon between the hours of 4 and 6 pm."

He wrote back "Mr George Bernard Shaw likewise."

Andante were delighted with the offer we made them, and along with Michael's very entertaining script, we put together some great songs for the show, which we called "Blowin' in the Wind".

Starting with Mr Tambourine Man, and going on through many Dylan greats to a grand finale of Knocking on Heaven's Door, it was a terrific presentation. We added some Joni Mitchell and Joan Baez, and put in Andante's request of Lennon and McCartney's All You Need is Love. This moved Heaven's Door back to being "false tabs" (when a show seems to be over but there's still an encore to come), and then Andante would come back on stage for All You Need is Love, as a rousing singalong finish.

We went up to Birmingham five times in all to rehearse, hiring a working men's club near to where Vee and Mark lived. Finally, we were happy with the whole thing. Michael had written a mix of entertaining banter for them to perform between the songs, and we'd made a powerpoint presentation of slides to project onto a big screen at the back of the stage, telling the story of Dylan and the other songwriters we featured.

17 theatres took the show and we opened in Penzance, going on eventually to Dundee (!) and finally ending up at Llanelli, again a theatre Michael and I had appeared at ourselves back in the nineties. A good venue and a good choice for our swan song.

We were both very emotional when the curtain came down that last night in Llanelli as you can imagine. We'd booked a night at a hotel just a few yards from the theatre. With it being a Saturday night, we'd completely forgotten what it's like nowadays to stay on a Saturday night in a British town centre. Our show finished at 10.30 and we were in bed in our room by 11.00, only to be kept awake until 3 am by the continuous, mindless thumping of a nearby disco. What a way to end a music tour!

Never mind. That was the last of our music shows, but we still had one final Dickens tour to take us to the very, very end.

<u>2017</u>

There was another substantial increase in rail fares, something that had become an annual event, and was quite a contrast with the freezing of fuel tax duty.

The Queen celebrated her Sapphire Jubilee. She'd now reigned for 65 years, making her the longest serving monarch in UK history.

There were several more terrorist attacks in London, including a major attack by Khalid Masood who ploughed through the pedestrians on Westminster Bridge before stabbing a policeman to death. Another Islamist extremist detonated a huge bomb at Manchester Arena at a concert by Ariana Grande, a young pop singer who appealed to teenage girls. He killed 23 and wounded another 139, most of them children.

The new 12 sided £1 coin was introduced, and there was a terrible fire at Grenfell Tower with 71 fatalities.

Tim Farron resigned as Liberal Leader over an apparent mismatch between his own personal view of Christianity and his party's view of certain issues. He was replaced by Sir Vince Cable.

The Duke of Edinburgh retired from public duty.

We lost disc-jockey Brian Matthew (radio's Saturday Club and tv's Thank Your Lucky Stars) and legendary entertainer Sir Bruce Forsyth. Known in recent years for his game shows, "Here they are, they're so appealing, come on dollies, do your dealing!", he'd been a great all-rounder. He could do lots of things a little bit. (Is that fair?) He could sing, he could tap dance, he could tell jokes, he could interview, he could do impersonations. He even appeared in a couple of big Hollywood movies, "Star!" with Julie Andrews, and "Bedknobs and Broomsticks" with Angela Lansbury.

The first time I saw him was in 1968 with my parents at the Mayflower Theatre, Southampton, then still the Gaumont. He picked on several women in the front row including my mother Muriel. He didn't quite get her name right and kept referring to her as "Meriel". Whenever a line didn't go down as well as he'd hoped, he'd say "Is that all right with you Meriel?" It was his one-man show, so he was on his own for the whole evening, accompanied by a large, very polished orchestra. When he asked for song requests, he told musical

director Don Hunt "'Meriel wants 'In a Monastery Garden'...
only trouble is, she can't get over the wall!"

When one of his comedy routines was starting to run out of
steam, he said "We'll be all right. Meriel's got a bottle of gin
in her handbag".

Michael and I saw him at The London Palladium in the mid
nineties and his act was still the same, with every one of
those lines I've just quoted.

We were at one of the dates on his final tour in 2015 when
he picked on a woman in the front row, saying "Sandra
wants 'In a Monastery Garden'... only trouble is she can't get
over the wall." Later he quipped "We'll be all right. Sandra's
got a bottle of gin in her handbag." This time, we were sitting
in Row W. He came running up the aisle to those of us at the
back saying "When the revolution comes, you lot will all be
sitting up the front." Then he looked around at us in the
cheap seats and added "These are my people! Common! I
can smell the crisps!"

<u>2018</u>

There was the biggest rise in rail fares for five years, and the
government re-nationalised rail services on the East Coast
Main Line.

London's murder rate now surpassed that of New York.

Salisbury was rocked by the poisoning of a former Russian
double agent and his daughter, with Russian involvement
said to be the "only plausible explanation".

Three more major high street chains went into administration – Toys R Us, Maplin Electronics, and HMV.

Tolls were finally scrapped on the Severn Bridge. We'd spent a fortune on tolls at around £8 a time every time we played a theatre in Wales. Now we'd finished, it was free!

There were numerous protests trying to overturn the result of the referendum, and various "deals" were tried and defeated. News was nothing but Brexit every day.

Ken Dodd died at the age of 90.

"How tickled I am, missus! What a beautiful day for stuffing a cucumber through the vicar's letterbox and shouting 'The Martians have landed!'"

If you imagine Ken telling this next gag, maybe you won't mind so much that it's so politically incorrect!

"On our 25th anniversary I told my wife I'd take her to a south sea island. She said 'That's wonderful. What will you do for our 50th?' I said I'll come and collect you."

After Ken had been cleared in court of tax evasion in a case brought by HMRC, Jimmy Tarbuck said "Ken Dodd is so old, he remembers when income tax was sixpence in the pound. Trouble was, he thought it still is."

Ken was a committed Christian and a staunch Catholic. He'd lived in the same small house in Knotty Ash, Liverpool all his life. Just a day or so before his death, he finally married the love of his life, Anne Jones. She'd been at his side all along, taking copious notes in the wings recording which jokes had gone well and which had not. She sold the souvenirs in the foyer everywhere they went, and on some occasions had a tiny cameo role in the show.

Singer Teddy Johnson died at the age of 98, and his wife Pearl Carr passed away at the same age not long after. They' both been living at Brinsworth House in their declining years. This is a retirement home at Twickenham for people in the profession. We used to go to their annual garden party and other events. At the last one we went to, I spotted Danny La Rue sitting alone on a bench at the edge of the lawn, looking forlorn. I went up to him and we chatted for a while. He was really pleased to see me. We hadn't met since the final show he did for us at the Lichfield Garrick. He gave me a new business card giving his address and his name "Danny Patrick Carroll", saying "I'm not Danny La Rue any more." I found this very touching, and then he added "I was good at my job, wasn't I?" He died just a few months later.

A very different event was the Churches Together England Conference at Derby, which I attended as the Dorset Delegate. There were 300 of us and we were all on the list in alphabetical order, so I was amused to see my name "Webb, Christopher" and then next BELOW mine "Welby, Justin"!

Stage Nine: Retirement?

In which we "downsize" to a lovely flat, and start to live more simply, but still "adventurously".

<u>2019</u>

Several more high street chains collapsed into administration including Debenhams following on the heels of House of Fraser, Jamie Oliver's restaurant group, travel agent Thomas Cook, and Mothercare.

726 homeless people died, a 22% increase since 2017.

In a sign of what is undoubtedly to come, we had the warmest February day on record, quickly followed by the hottest ever Easter Monday. Later in the year, the hottest June day was recorded, and then the hottest July. There were more than 100 flood warnings in the midlands and the north.

Theresa May announced a new legally-binding target to reach net zero greenhouse gas emissions by 2050. We were the first major industrialised nation to have such a goal – but it seems an awfully long way away.

There were demonstrations regarding climate change, which quickly turned to violence and anarchy.

Daily Brexit wranglings continued. The Lib Dems announced they would scrap Brexit without a second referendum if they won the next election, which seemed unlikely to say the least. In fact, when the election came, new leader Jo Swinson lost her seat.

All memories of Sandie Shaw and her win with "Puppet on a String" were long gone when we came LAST in the Eurovision Song Contest with just 11 votes. Mind you, there may have been one or two essential differences between this year's and our songs of the past. We still remember Cliff's "Congratulations" and Pearl and Teddy's "Sing Little Birdie". In 50 years' time, will everyone remember this year's British offering "Bigger Than Us" sung by Michael Rice?

Michael Rice?

Theresa May resigned and was replaced by Boris Johnson who finally held the General Election on my birthday, 12 December. Conservatives won a landslide victory with a majority of 80 seats, and Labour under Jeremy Corbin and John Mc Donnell had their worst result since 1935. Numerous all-time Labour strongholds in the north fell to the Tories for the first time in history.

We lost talented actor Albert Finney ("Murder on the Orient Express", "Annie", "Scrooge"), and sultry, seductive singer Scott Walker. A reclusive, troubled and terribly handsome man, Scott was a great favourite of my cousin Jenny - and me. Probably both for the same reason!

2019 was the year we moved once again. Our house at West Moors had five bedrooms, several reception rooms and a large outbuilding. The grounds were a third of an acre. We needed all this when we were running our business. Now we didn't need it any more. It was rapidly becoming a millstone round our necks. We decided to sell and to move to a flat.

After five months of endless problems and setbacks, we finally moved into a really lovely flat in West Parley, Ferndown. We're just six miles north of Bournemouth town centre, with buses to take us there in 25 minutes. It's just 20 minutes to Bournemouth Station, and 25 minutes the other way to Wimborne.

As it turned out, moving house was not the most traumatic event of the year.

Just three days after the move, my brother Peter passed away. He had been declining for many years, suffering from Parkinsons Disease, like his uncle Eric, and my dear friend, tv producer Barry Brown.

Michael and I visited Peter numerous times at the "home" where he lived out his final years at Netley, near Southampton. Peter's wife Barbara was endlessly attentive, visiting almost every day, and Rachel and Nina his two daughters, and Joe, Jack and Lexie, his three grandchildren were very caring. However, his decline was inexorable. Finally, he was taken into Southampton General Hospital where I managed to see him and exchange a few words. As it turned out I was the last person he ever spoke to.

We'd been through so much together, selling over 100 000 copies of our Tables Disco, working with advertising agencies, PR firms, even exhibiting at London's Ideal Home Exhibition, and the Birmingham equivalent at the NEC.

We'd lost both our parents, and dealt with the wills, probate etc. together. Now, of the four of us in our little family, I was the only one left.

Michael and I had been several times to hear Peter playing his keyboard at various clubs and hotels. I am left with Peter's recording of his versions of various standards, "Coming Home".

They say the trauma of moving house is right up at the top of the list, and a bereavement is right up there too. To have both in the space of three days is not something I would recommend.

There were two funerals in 2019 brought about by Parkinsons Disease. My brother's, and also Barry Brown's. I travelled to London to pay my final respects to Barry, along with many of his BBC colleagues. Barry had managed to stay at home in his flat in the Brompton Road until just a fortnight before the end, with a live-in carer who was the most wonderful and devoted young man. In the afternoons, they watched Barry's huge collection of dvds together, everything from Gone with the Wind, to Psycho and Citizen Kane.

We couldn't be more pleased with the move to Ferndown. "Downsizing" has been quite cathartic, with getting rid of much surplus, etc. Now there are lovely grounds, but we don't need to maintain them. The hall and stairs are cleaned once a week, but we don't need to clean them. There's a lift, and we're on the second floor. We have three bedrooms instead of our former five, but still two bathrooms – the secret of marital bliss!

<u>2020</u>

The first year of the new decade takes me to "three score years and ten".

2020 began with the death of our beautiful little hamster, Holly. She was our 11th. Over the years we've been to Malta eleven times, and we've owned eleven hamsters! They are the most lovely little creatures, and we've had a succession of females which we've called Hayley, Harriet, Hermione, Hilary, etc. The sad thing is that each one only lives about two years. Holly had lived longer than most, to nearly two and a half, and then she became ill with the hamster disease "wet tail". We think it might have been caused by the stress of moving to the flat at West Parley in Ferndown. Michael took her to the vet twice, but the treatment given didn't save her and she died late on New Year's Eve. Therefore, the New Year and the new decade began with us taking her to the woods to the east of Wimborne and leaving her there under a pile of leaves.

As I write, it is seventy years since 1950 when my story began. We are now living in an infantile kind of culture where BBC weather presenters address us as though we're 5 year olds, and products speak a-la Alice in Wonderland. Remember the little bottle on the glass table - "Drink Me"?

Now "refrigerate after opening", for example, has become "keep me in the fridge".

This is also the age of what is called "identity politics" whereby people speak on the basis of what particular tribe they consider they belong to.

The mangling of our once-great English language continues apace, particularly in the world of advertising where we now see slogans like "find your happy", "hello possible", or "shop everything home". Those are real examples. What are these slogans trying to promote? I have no idea.

Then I remember Tony Hancock telling us to go to work on an egg, or "drinkapintamilkaday" and I wonder whether anything has changed!

The general trend towards childishness in language accelerates. Breakfast, for example, is now "brekkie". Presents are "prezzies". Then there is text speak, where a word like "before" is now "B4".

What would my father think? I remember when I was a little boy asking him, "Can I have some more custard?"

He replied, "You certainly CAN, but the question is whether or not you MAY."

Every day for almost four years every news bulletin and every newspaper has carried stories and arguments about Brexit non-stop.

However, on 31 January this year, the first coronavirus cases were recorded in the UK. Now we have had many months of what has been called "lockdown" with everything shut. Michael and I have sat in our flat quietly reading day after day, going out for walks around the roads here in West Parley. We've discovered Poor Common, tucked away behind the houses, which is a joy. A nature reserve with tranquillity under the trees and a pond in the middle.

We had a bit of a hiatus during the summer, but now we're back in lockdown again.

We can't go to the theatre. All theatres are closed. You have to wear a mask to enter a shop, and "social distancing" is required everywhere, keeping two metres apart from other people. 50 000 people have died in the UK so far and the number of infections is rapidly increasing again as I write. We have entered the biggest recession since records began, with thousands of job losses, thousands of businesses made bankrupt, and no sign yet of a vaccine which could get us back to some semblance of normality.

We are now in a "second wave" of the virus that is being managed by different approaches in different parts of the UK. Hardship is greatly increasing, dozens of shops, restaurants, and pubs are closing never to re-open, and unemployment numbers are fast going back to levels not seen since the 80s.

2020 is proving to be quite a year.

The result of the USA election has been declared, with Joe Biden the winner. I was really moved by his inaugural speech. In this book I've quoted some of the best lines of the comedians of the past. Well, Mr Biden's best line was referring to the maps we've constantly been shown on television during the campaign. He said, "We've been seeing red states and blue states. I only see united states."

Meanwhile Mr Trump has separately declared that HE won, and will be starting legal action. Watch this space!

Des O'Connor has died at the ripe old age of 88. I first saw Des at the London Palladium in either 1970 or 71. It was while I was at college at Cheltenham and it was my first-ever visit to the world's greatest theatre. Being a student and not exactly flush with cash, I sat in The Gods as they call them. In other words, the Upper Circle. Wow, it's steep up there! There are no separate seats, only benches, and you're looking down from such a great height you see the tops of the performers' heads and just the very lowest bit of the backcloth. But at least I was there!

What would Dame Edna Everage say about the cheapest seats? "Cling on, possums! When you clap, only clap with one hand. Cling on with the other one!"

We all remember the long-lasting fictional feud between Eric Morecambe and Des O'Connor, whereby Eric would mock Des' singing and his ability as a performer in general. When Eric had his first heart attack, Des was performing at a theatre somewhere and asked his audience to pray for his friend. Once he'd recovered, Eric Morecambe appeared on the Parkinson show and spoke about Des doing that, saying "While I was in hospital, Des got his audience to pray for me. Isn't that wonderful? I'm feeling so much better now, and the prayers of those six or seven people will have made all the difference".

We have lost three greatly-valued gay friends. First, David Carter. He had been a very talented Musical Director who worked for us on many different productions. He was Musical Director for the pantomime in Norwich this year, but died part way through the run. We were unable to go to the funeral due to covid restrictions.

As Danny La Rue's musical director, David worked for us a lot. In Danny's shows every night Danny would refer to entertaining what he called the "SAGA generation", as his audience was always of a certain age!

David had to interrupt and call out "Danny! I've always wondered – what does SAGA mean exactly?" Back came Danny's answer. "It stands for Sex And Games for the Aged!"

Then, our local friend John Gibbs died. We invited him to lunch recently, along with another Friend, Bob Jacob. We had a great time, lots of laughs, and also much deep sharing of our respective journeys. We'd all been through the mill in similar ways. John was the garrulous one on that occasion, full of beans, full of stories.

The next day he sent an email to say what a lovely time they'd had. The day after that he died.

He was 76. Mercifully, we WERE able to go the funeral, a joint Anglican and Quaker Service, held at Bournemouth Crematorium for very limited numbers.

This week, a third gay friend has sadly passed away, Ian Willis. In some ways, Ian was Mr Wimborne. His house and garden were open to the public several times during the year. Now we hear he has died at home in his bath, having suffered a massive heart attack. I don't know who discovered his body, but it must have been a terrible shock.

As well as his public open days, Ian used to hold private parties twice a year "for gentlemen of a certain persuasion" as the invitation would say, to which Michael and I were always invited. There will be a big Memorial Service for Ian later in the year at the Minster.

Ian has left his house and garden to the Town, and they will be opened as a museum. His other property in Sidmouth will be sold, the proceeds going to the Priests House Museum. Michael and I had stayed at Ian's Sidmouth flat a few years ago, and he invited us to go again the last time I spoke to him, just a few months ago. Not to be. Make hay while the sun shines.

I find I am deeply moved by the death and loss of my friend, Ian Willis. He led a good life in many ways in the service of others but, as a gay man of that era, he never found true love. He did great work on the Dorset LGBT Switchboard, helping and counselling men in distress over having to come to terms with their sexuality or, more often, having to come to terms with the way others were treating them.

This was the year we lost another "national treasure", Dame Vera Lynn, who had reached her 103rd birthday. She is the only artiste in history to have had an album in the Chart at the age of 100. During the emergency coronavirus lockdown I've just described, the Queen gave an unprecedented mid-year television message in which she said "we WILL meet again".

Roy Hudd also recently died, along with local Wimborne actor Michael Medwin, and well-known personality Nicholas Parsons. Michael and I encountered Nicholas Parsons at Salisbury Playhouse one time. We'd seen him in the wonderful West End musical Charlie Girl in 1986 with Hollywood legend Cyd Charisse and others. I asked him what memories he had of that production and he retorted, "Cyd Charisse couldn't act. What more do you want to know?"

Various showbiz colleagues have always described Nicholas as being "difficult", a polite term that can cover a multitude of sins, as we discovered many times!

What can I record as good news? Certainly, the internet has given us easy access to information that would have been an effort to find before. Rail timetables, hotel bookings, theatre performance schedules, etc. are all available with a few clicks.

Also, trying to be positive, I think people are considering the environment much more. Supermarkets are starting to reduce plastic packaging, plastic carrier bags, general waste, etc. Rail lines are being electrified and we are moving towards electric cars instead of patrol or diesel. Much more needs to be done, however. The pace is too slow, but a good start has been made. The tv programmes Springwatch and Autumnwatch are a great joy, where we can see positive initiatives re the landscape and threatened species. We look forward with hope to the UK hosting a major climate conference next year in Glasgow.

I have been a businessman. The whole mindset of running a business and trying to make enough profit to live comfortably has always been my way. However, there's a medium in all things and we have hugely magnified inequality now, with footballers being paid millions, tv presenters being paid similarly and now, just a few people worth BILLONS, which no one could possibly need in this life.

To quote Ephraim Levi in "Hello Dolly",

"Money is like manure. It's no use until you spread it around a little."

And then there's the prison service. Far too many people are in prison when there could have been alternative ways of dealing with their crime. Where is the restorative justice whereby the burglar would repair the damage they've caused, address the distress of their victims and repay their loss?

I am what's known as a floating voter. Over the years, I've voted for all three main parties. Then they disappoint me!

I've tried to keep this book light on the whole so I'll leave all that on one side and say ...

What advice would I give now I'm in my 70th year, and what advice have I taken?

Firstly, stop and smell the roses. I have always been very driven. In some ways it's a good thing I was, as we wouldn't be here now if I hadn't been. Recently, I've learned to appreciate balance much more. I've gained a deeper appreciation of nature, of quiet times and contemplation. In other words, living more simply.

Once for Michael and me it was drive to Harrogate on Monday, Aberystwyth on Tuesday, Exeter on Wednesday, Norwich on Thursday, etc. That was the way we had to lead our lives. Now we stay local. I use my bus pass, and if we do go anywhere, we enjoy it even more. We've just been to Lulworth Cove, and walked all the way up the coast path to look over Durdle Door.

My second piece of advice would be to live in the moment. We so often spend half our time thinking about the future, making plans or worrying, and then we spend the other half of our time going over the past, regretting things we did or said, or what we DIDN'T do. All the time, we're missing what is happening now!

As I reach my three score years and ten, I look back at all that I've written here and marvel at how much I've done. How on earth did I manage to fit it all in?

On my journey, what have I found that I like? And what have I learned?

In no particular order, I like North Wales, steam railways, walking in the Dorset countryside, intelligent newspapers, a good play in a proper theatre, looking at maps, old fashioned musicals, Carol Burnett, peace and quiet, Ravel's Bolero, Rodgers and Hammerstein, Lincolnshire, meditation and contemplation, Malta, walking and tracing old railways, Lucille Ball, crisp winter days, ducks and duck ponds, the Scottish Borderlands, Edinburgh, showbusiness biographies, the river Stour and the river Test, Brussels and Bruges, Murder She Wrote, The Nutcracker Suite, Columbo, hamsters, good red wines.

And then there's pasta and pizza, ice cream, chocolate, Danish pastries, Camembert, Red Leicester, Vintage Cheddar, and ... and ...

And what DON'T I like? Again, in no particular order of importance, loud noisy places, Rap "music", aggressive drivers, crowds, graffiti, litter, rudeness, Identity Politics, most of today's BBC, text messages, social media, seafood and offal, extremist opinions either left or right.

I hope you've noticed that my first list is longer than the second.

I've spent nearly 65 000 words writing about all that I've done, so I really should reflect on what I've NOT done!

I have never been to a football match. I have never been inside a betting shop. I have never ridden a bike.

I have never tried drugs. I have never smoked.

I have never been to Paris. I have never seen a James Bond film – or a Harry Potter one for that matter! (Did I say always a rebel?)

I have never eaten an egg. I know they're in cakes etc. but I've never eaten an egg as such, poached, fried or boiled.

In all my years in showbusiness, I never called anyone "darling".

And what have I learned?

I said earlier on that there were two people who were shining lights in my early life. The Church of England would encourage you to "let your light shine", and I've recently discovered the Quaker notion "let your life speak". To me, they're two different ways of saying the same thing. Not easy, and certainly something that I've constantly fallen short of. Nevertheless, a worthy aim at any age, even if you're fast approaching 70!

And then I've learned such a lot from Michael. He worked tirelessly driving our huge vans all over the country, loading and unloading in snow and rain, managing troupes of egotistical actors, singers, dancers etc. with good humour and forbearance. He came to understand stage lighting and sound so that he could liaise with all the technicians at each theatre we played, often dealing with some very difficult people. Michael is also a talented artist, yet modesty is one of his many qualities.

On the day we met, he asked me what makes me angry, and I replied without hesitation "Injustice". I would still give the same answer today.

I've learned that we all have a shadow side, and it's best to acknowledge it and come to terms with it. I certainly have shadow aspects which I'm only too acutely aware of, but I'm not intending to rehearse them here!

Being gay, however, is NOT my shadow. It has been a great blessing.

I quote Rabbi Lionel Blue, from his insightful autobiography "A Backdoor to Heaven" ...

"It was an older, wiser colleague, more conforming and heterosexual too, who told me to ponder the opportunities God had given me by being gay. Doing so in a silent chapel, I was overwhelmed by the riches I'd received and never regarded. Because I had been an underdog myself, I felt for outsiders. I too knew what it was like to have no place in the 'happy family' pictures."

Not long before he died, my brother Peter was reflecting on both our lives and comparing notes. Just the two of us were together, as we so often had been. He said there were many differences between our respective experiences. We had led extremely different lives. However, I was able to agree when he added "but above all, we both found love".

APPENDIX 1:
Sample children's/pantomime tour.

DEREK GRANT PRESENTS
Pinocchio

2000

Nov

4	Aberdare	Coliseum
5	Ebbw Vale	Beaufort Theatre
11	London	Hackney Empire Theatre
12	Thursford	Thursford Collection
18	Welshpool	Theatr Clera
19	Aberystwyth	Arts Centre

Dec

26-31	Ickenham	Compass Theatre

2001

Feb

17	Bradford	St George's Hall
18	Bishops Stortford	Rhodes Centre
19	Ealing	Town Hall

20	Stevenage	Gordon Craig Theatre
21	Ipswich	Corn Exchange
22	Bedworth	Civic Hall
23	Newark	Palace Theatre
24	Liverpool	Neptune Theatre
25	Heywood	Civic Hall

April

7	Hastings	White Rock Theatre
8	Lowestoft	Marina Theatre
9	Grays	Thameside Theatre
10	Tunbridge Wells	Assembly Hall
11	Reading	Concert Hall
12	Hull	New Theatre
17	Rhyl	Pavilion Theatre
18	Middleton	Civic Hall
19	Lichfield	Civic Hall
20-21	St Albans	Alban Arena

May

19	Basingstoke	Haymarket Theatre
26	Boston	Blackfriars Arts Centre
27	Helmsley	Old Meeting House

28	Scunthorpe	Plowright Theatre
29	Harlow	Playhouse
30	Sevenoaks	Stag Theatre
31	Hornchurch	Queen's Theatre

June

2	Horsham	Arts Centre

Oct

20	London	Stratford Circus
21	St Helens	Theatre Royal
22	Mablethorpe	Dunes Family Entertainment Centre
23	Oswaldtwistle	Civic Theatre
24	Haverhill	Arts Centre
25	Redhill	Harlequin Theatre
26	Ilford	Kenneth More Theatre
27	Clacton on Sea	West Cliff Theatre
28	Sutton	Secombe Theatre
29	Burgess Hill	Martletts Hall
31	Jersey	Opera House

Nov

1	Maidenhead	Magnet Leisure Centre
2	Hove	Centre
3	Weymouth	Pavilion Complex

2003

Aug

18-19	Jersey	Opera House
25-26	Jersey	Opera House

Oct

11	Chesterfield	Winding Wheel Theatre
12	Kendal	Leisure Centre
13	Stranraer	Ryan Centre
14	Kilmarnock	Palace Theatre
15	Lanark	Memorial Hall
16	Greenock	Arts Guild Theatre
17	Largs	Barrfields Pavilion
18	Liverpool	Neptune Theatre
25	Hunstanton	Princess Theatre
26	Skegness	Embassy Theatre
27	Worthing	Pavilion Theatre

28	Weston-Super-Mare	Playhouse
29	Hoddesdon	Broxbourne Civic Hall
30	Grays	Thameside Theatre
31	Winsford	Civic Hall

Nov

1	London	Hackney Empire Theatre
2	Abertillery	Community Theatre
16	Shanklin	Portico Theatre
20	Donaghmore	Bardic Theatre
21-22	Cookstown	Burnavon Arts Centre
24	Strabane	St Patrick's Hall
25	Tandragee	Leisure Centre
27	Armagh	Orchard Leisure Centre
28	Maghera	Recreation Centre
29	Carrickfergus	Leisure Centre

Dec

1-13	Belfast	Newtownabbey Courtyard Theatre
16	Skelmersdale	Phoenix Theatre
17	Leeds	Yorkshire Television Centre
18-19	Crewe	Danebank Theatre

20	Milton Keynes	Woughton Centre
23	Abergavenny	Borough Theatre
27	Ormskirk	Civic Hall
28	Oswestry	Leisure Centre
29	Consett	Empire Theatre
31	Crowthorne	Edgebarrow Sports Centre

2004

Jan

2-3	Halstead	Empire Theatre
6-9	Crewe	Danebank Theatre
10	Rendlesham	Angel Theatre

Feb

14	Potters Bar	Wyllyotts Centre
15	Buxton	Opera House
16	St Neots	Priory Centre
17	Bradford	St George's Hall
18	Blackpool	Grand Theatre
19	Hartlepool	Town Hall Theatre
20	Middlesbrough	Middlesbrough Theatre
21	Boston	Blackfriars Arts Centre

| 28 | Doncaster | Civic Theatre |
| 29 | Exmouth | Pavilion Theatre |

March

| 7 | Guernsey | St Peter Port St James' Arts Centre |
| 13-14 | St Albans | Arena |

April

6	Hornchurch	Queen's Theatre
7	Andover	Cricklade Theatre
9	Morecambe	Dome
10	Derby	Assembly Rooms
11	Clacton-on-Sea	West Cliff Theatre
12	Bognor Regis	Alexandra Theatre
13	Yeovil	Octagon Theatre
14	Haywards Heath	Clair Hall
15	Darwen	Library Theatre
16	Heywood	Civic Centre
17	Chapel St Leonards	Robin Hood Leisure Park
18	Bridgnorth	Theatre on The Steps

May

| 29 | Bedworth | Civic Hall |

30	New Brighton	Floral Pavilion
31	Sevenoaks	Stag Theatre

June

1	Port Talbot	Princess Royal Theatre
2	Porthcawl	Grand Pavilion Theatre
3	Pwllheli	Neuadd Dwyfor
5	Margate	Theatre Royal
6	Tamworth	Assembly Rooms

Oct

24	Colchester	Sir Charles Lucas Leisure Centre
25	Fleetwood	Marine Hall
26	Luton	Library Theatre
27	Bournemouth	Pavilion Theatre
28	Harlow	Playhouse
30	Swindon	Arts Centre
31	Bromyard	Conquest Theatre

Nov

6	Ipswich	Wolsey Theatre
7	Rendlesham	Angel Theatre

2007

Production re-cast at this point, now starring Don Maclean, and using Richard Gill's script.

Feb

10	Northwich	Memorial Hall
11	Bolton	Albert Halls
12-16	Lichfield	Lichfield Garrick Theatre

Sept

15	Bognor Regis	Alexandra Theatre
29	Cwmbran	Congress Theatre
30	Leamington Spa	Royal Spa Centre

Oct

14	Leeds	City Varieties Music Hall
20	Burgess Hill	Martletts Hall
22	Tamworth	Assembly Rooms
23	Chesham	Elgiva Theatre
24	Verwood	Verwood Hub
26	Skipton	Mart Theatre
28	Exmouth	Pavilion Theatre

2009

Oct

10	Ferndown	Barrington Theatre
11	Bognor Regis	Regis Centre
17	Boston	Blackfriars Theatre
24	St Helen's	Theatre Royal
25	New Brighton	Floral Pavilion Theatre
26	Darwen	Library Theatre
27-31	Lichfield	Garrick Theatre

Nov

1	Hertford	Castle Hall

APPENDIX 2:
Sample comedy/music tour.

DEREK GRANT PRESENTS
The Best of Joyce Grenfell

with Maria Gibbs as Joyce, and various pianists

2002

Oct

4	Doncaster	Civic Theatre
5	Halifax	Square Chapel Arts Centre
6	Wavendon	The Stables
12	Sheringham	Little Theatre
16	Alnwick	Playhouse
17	Whitehaven	Rosehill Theatre
27	Morecambe	The Platform
29	Cwmbran	Congress Theatre
31	Ebbw Vale	Beaufort Theatre

Nov

1	Newtown	Theatr Hafren

3	Wrexham	Rhosllanerchrugog Theatr Stiwt
4	Milford Haven	Torch Theatre
7	Ystradgynlais	The Welfare
9	Redditch	Palace Theatre
14	Northwich	Memorial Hall
15	Kings Lynn	Arts Centre
16	Andover	Cricklade Theatre
17	Tring	Court Theatre
19	Warwick	Bridge House Theatre
21	Torquay	Toads Theatre
22	Taunton	Brewhouse Theatre
23	Tavistock	The Wharf
26	Redhill	Harlequin Theatre
30	Lyme Regis	Marine Theatre

Dec

1	Hastings	White Rock Theatre
6	Norwich	Playhouse

2003

Jan

15	Wellingborough	Castle Theatre
19	South Shields	Customs House Theatre
31	Sevenoaks	Stag Theatre

Feb

1	Rickmansworth	Watersmeet Theatre
8	Hertford	Castle Hall
9	Clacton-on-Sea	West Cliff Theatre
11	Ipswich	Wolsey Theatre
13	East Grinstead	Chequer Mead Theatre
15	St Helens	Theatre Royal
19	Whitley Bay	Playhouse Theatre
20	Berwick-upon-Tweed	Maltings Arts Centre
21-22	Mussleburgh	Brunton Theatre
28	Shrewsbury	Music Hall

March

1	Newark	Palace Theatre
2	Chelmsford	Civic Theatre
4	Grantham	Guildhall Arts Centre

6	Margate	Theatre Royal
14	Camberley	Theatre
15	Trowbridge	Arc Theatre
19	Pontypridd	Muni Arts Centre
20	Ludlow	Assembly Rooms
21	Chester	Gateway Theatre
23	Douglas	Gaiety Theatre
28	Maidenhead	Norden Farm Arts Centre
30	Leeds	City Varieties Music Hall

April

2	Bridport	Arts Centre
5	Blackwood	Miners' Institute
9	Guernsey	St Peter Port St James' Hall
24	Ilfracombe	Landmark Theatre
25	Yeovil	Octagon Theatre
30	Bromsgrove	Festival

May

1	Brecon	Theatr Brycheiniog
2	Tamworth	Assembly Rooms
10	Fowey	Festival

10	Mansfield	Palace Theatre
14	Cheltenham	Bacon Theatre
15	Potters Bar	Wyllyotts Centre
16	Lincoln	Theatre Royal
24	Haverhill	Arts Centre
25	Christchurch	Regent Centre

June

19	Scunthorpe	Plowright Theatre
24	London	Chelsea Festival

Sept

13	Taunton	Brewhouse Theatre
28	Widnes	Queen's Hall

Oct

2	Bury St Edmunds	Theatre Royal
3	Herne Bay	King's Hall

Nov

14	Frome	Memorial Theatre
23	Leicester	Little Theatre

2004

Production re-cast at this point, now starring Caroline Fields, with David Carter at the piano.

Oct

| 30 | Worcester | Huntingdon Hall |

Nov

4	East Grinstead	Chequer Mead Arts Centre
19	Gainsborough	Trinity Arts Centre
28	Haywards Heath	Clair Hall

2005

Feb

| 19 | Lichfield | Garrick Theatre |

March

10	Margate	Theatre Royal
11	Sidmouth	Manor Pavilion Theatre
22	Yeovil	Octagon Theatre
23	Redhill	Harlequin Theatre
24	Shrewsbury	Music Hall

| 25 | Scunthorpe | Plowright Theatre |
| 27 | Lytham St Anne's | Lowther Pavilions Theatre |

April

1	Bedford	Corn Exchange
14	Potters Bar	Wyllyotts Centre
21	Wimborne	Tivloli Theatre

May

| 15 | Leeds | City Varieties Music Hall |
| 28 | Sevenoaks | Playhouse |

June

| 24 | Pershore | No. 8 Community Arts Centre |

Aug

| 23 | Colchester | Mercury Theatre |

Oct

6	Hartlepool	Town Hall Theatre
18	Chesterfield	Winding Wheel Theatre
27	Ebbw Vale	Beaufort Theatre

2007

Sept

12	Tamworth	Assembly Rooms
13	Cwmbran	Congress Theatre
19	Belfast	Newtownabbey Courtyard Theatre
24	Verwood	Verwood Hub

Oct

| 22 | Watton | Queen's Hall |
| 29 | South Shields | Customs House Theatre |

Nov

| 15 | Fareham | Ferneham Hall |
| 18 | Lichfield | Garrick Theatre |

2008

Jan

| 25 | Whitehaven | Rosehill Theatre |

June

| 19 | Tewkesbury | Roses Theatre |

2009

April

1	Norwich	Maddermarket Theatre
17	Wavendon	The Stables

APPENDIX 3: Sample Reviews.

Little Red Riding Hood, Weymouth Pavilion. Dorset Evening Echo.

"Pantomime Outshines Star Shows."

It is a sorry state of affairs when an off-season pantomime manages to put the majority of Christmas shows to shame, but that is what happens when The Derek Grant Organisation bring their shows to town. Little Red Riding Hood was an utter delight from start to finish. Simple, funny, packed with slapstick humour and good old-fashioned audience interaction, and at 90 minutes plus interval, a much more suitable length for its target audience than festive shows that often drag on interminably. There wasn't a slow moment – good family theatre that all ages could enjoy. And enjoy it they did. The younger end of the audience revelled in the tomfoolery, while the older end had enough double-entendres to keep them amused. It was excellent, honest, hard-working, no-frills entertainment, and frankly I'd rather have that any day of the week than a host of "big names" coasting on their egos, and leaving their audience distinctly underwhelmed.

--

Danny La Rue Music Hall, Camberley Theatre.   The Stage.

"Glossy, well-produced music hall show."

It is fashionable nowadays in some quarters to knock the phenomenon that is Danny La Rue, yet few entertainers in Britain have consistently stayed at the top for so long. Now at an age when most female impersonators would be happy to hang up their bras, the 77 year old is back on the road in a glossy, well-produced music hall production. True, La Rue may not be giving a high-kick these days, but the bosom is just as opulent, and the dresses just as spectacular. His brand of ultra-glamorous vulgarity always proved to be catnip to coach parties and family audiences, and the largely female audience at Camberley were not disappointed as he led them through bawdy choruses of music hall songs interspersed with gags about Clare Short and Tony Blair. A selection of songs from La Cage Aux Folles and Hello Dolly was also a poignant reminder of this unique performer's versatility. The production is ably compered by Spencer K Gibbins, and among the supporting acts is chirpy Andy Eastwood who plays a mean banjo and violin, plus youngster Lorrie Brown who pays tribute to Vera Lynn. It is unlikely that the war-torn Dame Vera ever sang to the troops in a mauve evening dress and high heels, but Brown delivers the vocals well. Another touch of vocal nostalgia is the appearance of David and Pauline Conway, one of variety's most polished acts. Excellent musical direction is by David Carter.

--

The Best of Joyce Grenfell,
Lichfield Garrick Theatre.
Lichfield Mercury.

"Mistress of the Monologue."

The Lichfield Garrick was transformed into the world of Joyce Grenfell to the delight of the capacity audience in this tribute to an outstanding entertainer of the English stage. Caroline Fields knew her character well. It was not only the costumes and high-heeled shoes that helped to captivate the image of the original Joyce, it was the attention to detail, the absolute perfect pronunciation of every word, which was a characteristic of Grenfell herself. The well-loved signature tune captured the mood of the evening. Caroline had her audience completely on board in the first sketch. The great gift of this artiste, as was that of Joyce herself, was to change character and mood with enormous skill. In the first three numbers she smoothly moved from a nursery school teacher to the chairwoman of a northern choral society, and then to a moving glimpse of a mother seeing her family off on a boat train as they were about to emigrate, trying unsuccessfully to keep the British stiff upper lip. All good things come to an end, but not until we had been treated to twenty sketches in a one-woman show. A great evening, great memories, and a great performer in Caroline Fields.

APPENDIX 4:
International artistes seen on stage.

Some I can remember include … Frank Sinatra, Ginger Rogers, Andy Williams, Jack Benny, Tony Bennett, Bob Hope, Johnny Mathis, Rosemary Clooney, Michael Feinstein, Julie Andrews, Tommy Steele, Petula Clark, Liberace, Carol Burnett, Carol Channing, Debbie Reynolds, Chita Riveira, Liza Minnelli, Lorna Luft, Anthony Newley, Lucie Arnaz, Tyne Daly, Cyd Charisse, Bob Dylan, Diana Ross, Dionne Warwick, Sammy Davis Jnr, Elaine Strich, Beatrice Arthur, Joan Collins, Rue Maclanahan, David Frost, Jim Dale, Mickey Rooney, Ann Miller, Angela Lansbury, Maurice Chevalier, Barry Humphries, Joan Armatrading, Joan Baez, Eartha Kitt, Neil Sedaka, Barbara Cook, George Hearn, and others. Most of these Michael and I saw together, and a few we met.

APPENDIX 5:
UK artistes seen on stage.

Amongst others, I remember ... Morecambe and Wise, Mike Yarwood, Val Doonican, Susan Maughan, Paul Daniels and Debbie Magee, Max Bygraves, Bruce Forsyth, Des O'Connor, Jimmy Tarbuck, Frankie Howerd, Tommy Cooper, Russ Conway, Cilla Black, Frankie Vaughan, Dick Emery, Ronnie Corbett, Ronnie Barker, Larry Grayson, Dora Bryan, Anita Harris, Lulu, Tom O'Connor, Ken Dodd, Eric Sykes, Hattie Jacques, Jimmy Edwards, Sandy Powell, Dickie Henderson, Billy Dainty, Cliff Richard, Pearl Carr and Teddy Johnson, Pam Ayres, Joe Longthorne, Arthur Askey, Roy Hudd, Leslie Crowther, Bobby Crush, Joe Mr Piano Henderson, Roy Castle, Mrs Mills, Malcolm Roberts. Many of these I saw before Michael, and many of these I met.

APPENDIX 6:
Professional theatre booking terms.

The theatre manager I met at that first conference at Southport explained all the various terms that theatres use to book shows. In order, they are as follows:-

The best for the venue is for the producer to hire it for the show. The venue charges a fee, and you get all the ticket sales (if there are any!) Suppose you pay £3000 to hire the theatre. Even then, it's not so simple as that. You've probably paid another £2000 to your artistes, plus you've spent on everything from poster printing to hotel rooms. If you're not very careful and you don't know what you're doing, your loss is likely to be £3000 to £4000 at least. The venue have made their money in the fee they charged you, your artistes have made their money in the fees you've paid them. It's just you - the producer - whose bank balance is several thousand lower. We almost never did this in our career, but you've got to earn yourself a reputation before venues will trust you enough to offer more attractive terms.

The best arrangement for the producer is a Guarantee. Here, you cost up your show to include your artiste fees and all the ancillary expenses you'll incur. Let's say it comes to £3500 per performance. You charge the venue a guarantee of £4500. You will therefore make £1000 profit. Most of our shows were on this basis.

The middle way is a split. We also did lots of these over the years, and more and more towards the end when times were not what they once were. Typically, the terms are 75/25. Here everyone is taking a risk (except the artistes who'll get their fixed fees whether anyone goes to the show or not). The Producer will get 75% of box office takings, and the venue will keep 25% and they'll get all their bar takings, ice creams, etc. as well. We would get programme sales.

Finally, there's a First Call, which takes us back to that helpful theatre manager I met at Southport. We did these as well sometimes. Here the Producer will get slightly better terms than a straight percentage split. Suppose you cost up your show at £3500 per performance. You're offered a First Call on £5000. This doesn't mean you'll make a profit of £1500. For that, you need a Guarantee. A First Call means you'll get all the ticket sales up to £5000. If ticket sales amount only to £3000, that's all you'll get, and in this example, that's £500 less than the show has cost you, so again a risk.

Printed in Great Britain
by Amazon